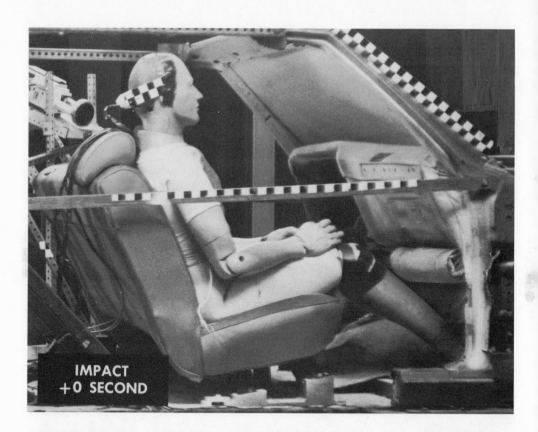

IMPACT
+0 SECOND

IMPACT
+2/30 SECOND

IMPACT
+1/30 SECOND

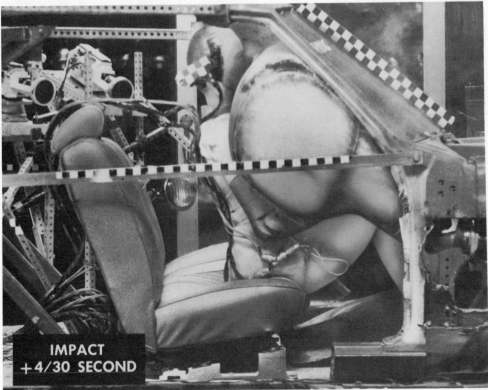

IMPACT
+4/30 SECOND

IT'S SMART TO USE A DUMMY

WESTMINSTER PRESS BOOKS

BY

SUZANNE HILTON

How Do They Get Rid of It?
How Do They Cope with It?
It's Smart to Use a Dummy

IT'S SMART
TO USE A DUMMY

by
SUZANNE HILTON

THE WESTMINSTER PRESS
Philadelphia

688.1
H656 2

ISBN 0–664–32500–9

LIBRARY OF CONGRESS CATALOG CARD No. 78–155902

BOOK DESIGN BY
DOROTHY ALDEN SMITH

PUBLISHED BY THE WESTMINSTER PRESS
PHILADELPHIA, PENNSYLVANIA ®

PRINTED IN THE UNITED STATES OF AMERICA

CONTENTS

INTRODUCTION

Ever been called a dummy? Rejoice! Dummies are a very select group.

Everyone uses dummies at some time in life—usually without knowing it. Dummies keep people from getting hurt, make their lives more comfortable, take their medicine for them, do their boring jobs, teach them, play with them, sell their products, test their machines, even save their lives.

Some of the dummies you may expect to find are not here. Football tackling dummies, ventriloquists' dummies (another whole book), artist's dummies (rarely used now) never made it into these pages. When the doors were opened a flood of dummies appeared in answer to the call of "Hey, dummy!" Decision of the judges was based on originality and limited to dummies not related to the author or publishers.

Even among dummies, there are the Very Important People and the little guys, the ones who work hard and the ones that just sit around, the pretty ones and the uglies. Some cost $150 and some are $40,000. Some have straw stuffing and some have computer brains.

Some are called dummies, but others go by names such as phantoms, torsos, models, dolls, anthropomorphic dummies, and mechanical analogs. The fashion world calls them *mannequins,* but science uses *manikins.* In a medical school library, they are listed under "Models, Structural."

No matter what the name, they are all dummies. And they share a common aim—to act as substitutes for the living.

They fearlessly volunteer for jobs no person would have—testing new parachutes, tumbling over a cliff, getting shot out of a space capsule, rolling end over end in a car, romping through a 2200°F. fire. They take jobs that would soon bore a mortal to death—posing for days in shop windows, standing for years in museums, chasing crows from farm fields. They get operated on, resuscitated, orbited, radiated, folded, spindled, and mutilated.

It's a greater life—for people. The world is safer, more attractive, and more comfortable for everyone because dummies helped make it that way. Here's how they did it.

1

History from Dummies

PERMANENT PEOPLE

I**N THE EARLY** damp hours of a March morning in 1547, every candle in the castle of Rambouillet was burning. The king, François I, had planned to go hunting this day—but now he was dead. It was time for the duty that Clouet, the king's portrait painter, had dreaded most. Since his appointment as painter and royal valet de chambre, Clouet had enjoyed all the privileges that honor had carried with it. But all the time, in the back of his mind, he had known there would come this last personal service he must perform for his king.

First, there was the death mask to make. Clouet hurried to the bedside of the dead king as soon as the new king had left his father's room. He put the wet plaster on the king's face and over both hands. The plaster set quickly and soon, with a few deft taps, it could be removed. Clouet took it to his studio, hoping the mask would not show how much his king had suffered these last years. He poured hot wax into the plaster molds and let it cool. Then he separated the wax face from the plaster and carefully studied its features.

Clouet took his oil colors and began adding tint to the pale wax. He painted the king's eyes open. After all, he was not supposed to look dead. People who looked on this face must recognize their king as he looked in life. Then the face mask was attached to a waxen head. Reaching up to his top shelf, he took down a sturdy wooden box. He unlocked it and tenderly felt the bits of hair he had collected from the floor of the king's chamber after every haircut and beard-trimming. Painstakingly, one strand at a time, Clouet inserted the hair into the wax.

Helpers in another part of the castle were weaving a mannequin out of wicker reeds, measuring carefully to be sure it was the exact size of the king's body. When it was finished, the effigy was clothed in a shirt of fine Dutch linen and covered over with silken garments that had been put away for this solemn occasion. After the mannequin was dressed in the ermine coronation robe, the head was

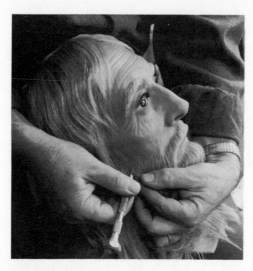

A wig specialist implants a beard—one strand at a time

attached. But Clouet was not finished yet. There were still two more mannequins to make.

Sadly the old painter took the two small death masks that had been made earlier. This one of the young dauphin had been waiting eleven years. The other, that of the young Duke of Orleans, had been made quite hurriedly when the boy died of the plague just eighteen months earlier. The new king had decreed that the two brothers should share the funeral of their father —an honor they had earned twenty years before when their father had been a prisoner in Spain. The cruel Spanish king had decided to free François I, but the price of his freedom was to exchange him for his two small sons. François had not rested until he was able to buy his sons' freedom from Spain. But prison had left its mark on both boys. They had died not long afterward and were buried in tombs miles from each other. Now at last all three would be together at the Abbey of St. Denis.

Making effigies took a long time, and almost two months had gone by before Clouet was satisfied that his figures looked the way he wanted them to look. For François I, there were two sets of hands—one set for the long journey to Paris and another set, with fists clenched, to hold the scepter later on. Now the richly dressed mannequins were laid on the three coffins and a solemn processional started out for Notre Dame about forty miles away.

Many ceremonies were held in the Paris cathedral before the effigies of the king and his sons were finally carried to St. Denis, the traditional burial place for French kings. When the bodies were buried, the mannequins were taken to the sacristy and placed beside the waxen images of former kings.

Just before the French Revolution (almost 250 years later), a German traveler said that he had visited St. Denis and had seen the whole "succession of French kings, life size, modeled in wax, robed in red and sitting on chairs with sceptres and crowns." Such a collection of royal symbols was bound to attract rebel fanatics. Vowing to destroy St. Denis, the revolutionists attacked the abbey. The ermine-clad mannequins paid the price for being associated with royalty, but they served their kings to the end. The mob tore the dummies to bits. Then the dummies and their kings were burned in a huge fire. But the abbey was spared.

Being buried is the least popular of all human customs—especially for the person to be buried. And kings were no exception. While they lived, they had been able to fend off their enemies. But they all worried about what their enemies might do when they got their chance. As it turned out, many of them found a dummy for the job.

The ancient Egyptian pharaohs and nobles were especially concerned about losing their bodies. They believed in life after death and that included using the same bodies. They were taking no chances on being less than a nobleman when they returned. But they also believed that the soul flitted around freely for a while, returning to the body when it was ready. Therefore, there must be a body for it to go into. They plotted their tombs secretly with blind alleys and booby-trapped passageways. Often secret rooms held only a mannequin of a dead noble. In many cases, the real body has never been found to this day.

Kings were deeply concerned about what happened to them after death. If a mannequin could be made to take the brunt of their enemies' hatred, so much the better. It was the custom in England to carry the monarch to his burial in full view of the people. This way there would be no danger of a pretender showing up at a later date and claiming to be the king. But the kings wanted their own bodies buried

quickly and quietly. The rest of the job—the processionals and lying-in-state—was gladly turned over to the mannequins.

Edward III died in 1377 a good distance from London on a hot summer day. Stoically, the men unfortunate enough to be chosen his pallbearers trudged miles carrying the king, the coffin, and his mannequin. No flimsy wax figure for Edward III! His mannequin was carved from the trunk of an oak tree. The figure had to be hollowed out in the back to make it light enough to lift off the ground. The oaken Edward III rests today in the old Norman undercroft of Westminster Abbey in company with the waxen mannequins of Elizabeth I, Charles II, the Duchess of Buckingham, and some of her children. After lying on a catafalque for years, the dummies were put in glass cases. But evidently not soon enough, for caretakers at the Abbey refer to them as "the ragged regiment."

Oliver Cromwell, who relieved England's Charles I of his head as well as his throne, was taking no chances when he died on September 3, 1658. He was buried almost at once. But his son was finding it not so easy to step into his father's shoes. Just to remind people of his father's power, he kept Cromwell's mannequin lying around, dressed in royal robes and bearing a crown and scepter, for three months longer.

Frederick II, king of Prussia, really had a thing about dummies. When his father, Frederick William I, died in 1740, he said he did not want any fuss made over him. Frederick II knew what his father was worried about, so he buried him quickly. But about the fuss—Frederick II had other ideas. After taking two weeks to get everything ready, he invited all the nobility to see his father lying in state. Filing first through a "mourning chamber," they were startled to see a dummy of the old king sitting up completely dressed in an armchair. Then they entered the bedchamber where another dummy of the dead king lay, surrounded by guards and candles. After a gloomy funeral, the dummy was buried with due ceremony. Evidently Frederick II thought the whole show a great success, because years later when he died, a dummy was buried in his place too.

It took a murder to get wax mannequins out of the morbid rut they were in and into the field of education and entertainment. Jean Paul Marat was one of the bloodiest of the French Revolutionists, with a long list of enemies and a short list of friends. He had sent thousands of Frenchmen to the guillotine. Then one day a girl, Charlotte Corday, stabbed him to death while he was taking a bath. Naturally his enemies wanted to see the body to be sure he was good and dead. He could not be placed on view, because he had leprosy, and photography had not been invented, so there was nothing else to do—except call on a mannequin. The wax sculptor did

get a bit carried away, picturing a bloodcurdling scene of Marat in the act of being stabbed. Most people found the waxwork horrible, but they came to look all the same. One lady came away thinking that wax mannequins should have something to offer to an audience that was not bloodthirsty.

Mme. Tussaud had learned to model in wax from her uncle, a Swiss wax sculptor. During the French Revolution, she lived dangerously in Paris, where she was suspected of having sympathy with the royalist side. After some time in prison, she escaped to

A rotund pilgrim's urethane foam stomach is filed down

WAX MUSEUM ENTERPRISES, LYNCH DISPLAY CORP.

London. There, in 1802, she opened a "different" kind of waxwork exhibit.

Most of Mme. Tussaud's figures of important people were modeled from life—because she knew many important people. She dreamed of her mannequins showing generations of children how these people had really looked. A trip to Madame Tussaud's Wax Museum in the 1800's was an education in an age when even history books rarely had more than a few drawings in them. There were no movies or television to help a child see what life was like "in the old days." There were not even any photographs yet. Men carried tiny colored wax "portraits" enclosed in small leather cases to remember how their loved ones looked. Now these portraits in wax were growing into full-size, three-dimensional portraits.

Most early U.S. museums found room for a few wax figures among the hodgepodge of ornaments from a Hindu temple, a moth-eaten bird, a jar of gallstones and an unlabeled collection of seashells from the Pacific. These were the years of exploration and travel. Even the tired and dusty American settler had a thirst for knowledge about the rest of the world. Some traveling exhibits included wax figures of the Incas of Peru or of royal families from obscure parts of Europe, complete with fake jewels.

But children living near Cincinnati, Ohio, in the years just before the Civil War must have been the best-behaved children in the world. At least

Harriet Tubman lives again in wax
AMERICAN WAX MUSEUM, PHILADELPHIA

temporarily. A mechanical and waxwork horror of the worst sort gave them a personal glimpse into the underworld regions that waited for sinners. Preachers took their flocks and groups of children from Sunday school to see "Dante's Inferno." It made more impression than all the preaching they could do on what they believed might happen to a sinner. There were screams, shrieks, groans, clanking chains, hissing snakes, and crashing thunderbolts. Grotesque figures writhed and reached out toward the

13

terrified spectators. In case any of the patrons were daring enough to touch the mechanical marvels, the "King of Terrors" (played by the owner himself) reached out with his magic wand to give them a slight electric shock.

Today most wax museums specialize in the figures of people who brought fame to their own area. While Philadelphia and Washington, D.C., feature the great people in American history, Gettysburg shows the men connected with that Civil War battlefield. Plymouth, Massachusetts, tells the story of the Pilgrims in wax scenes. Hollywood's wax museum re-creates the greatest scenes from motion pictures. Over twenty-five wax museums in the United States and Canada each cover entirely different subjects.

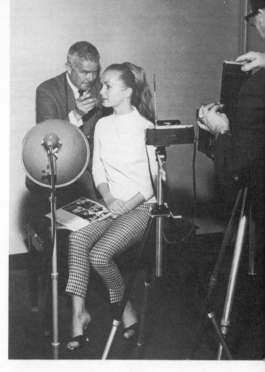

Debbie Reynolds sits for exacting facial measurements and 3-D color photographs before she is immortalized in wax as "The Singing Nun"

MOVIELAND WAX MUSEUM, BUENA PARK, CALIF.

Massasoit's Treaty lasted peacefully for forty years, but these treaty makers will have a much longer life

WAX MUSEUM ENTERPRISES, LYNCH DISPLAY CORP.

When a museum plans to do a figure of someone now famous it sends out a questionnaire to be filled in by that person or by someone close to him. The questions ask height, weight, complexion, color of hair and eyes, distinguishing features, and anything else the person may feel is important to make a true copy of himself. John Glenn even enclosed a lock of his blond hair. Henry Ford sent his 1916 driver's license so the museum would know his description during that year.

A detailed, life-sized figure is then sculptured in clay over a frame. The sculptor must be certain every wrinkle and muscle that he wants showing on the finished dummy is perfect on the

14

clay model. By the time he makes his clay dummy, he has plans on his desk for the entire scene—where each dummy will stand and in what position, what props will be needed, and how the background will look. He keeps a supply of completed hands available, so that if at the last minute he needs a clutching hand to carry a pail or a clenched fist to show anger, he will not have to make it in a rush.

Plaster molds are made from the clay figure if the dummy is to be made in wax. But dummies made of a vinyl plastisol must have a mold made from heat-resistant material. Since a half-dressed Indian figure shows so much "skin area," he looks better made of vinyl. After the casting is removed from the mold, it is time for the final touches of hair, eyes, and coloring. In another part of the workshop, the

Kirk Douglas does a double take, seeing his waxen twin about to battle a fellow gladiator in a scene from Spartacus
MOVIELAND WAX MUSEUM, BUENA PARK, CALIF.

Not many stars have to put on waders to see themselves up close as Cliff Robertson does in a scene from PT 109, *in which he portrays former President John F. Kennedy—in wax*
MOVIELAND WAX MUSEUM, BUENA PARK, CALIF.

bodies are made. A metal rod fits into the body and through the neck to secure the head. Arms are made almost to the wrist and then the molded wax hands are added. A tailor measures the completed dummy for his set of new—or historical—clothes.

Wax dummies are fragile. They will crack in extreme cold or melt in too much heat. Nor can they be exposed to the sun. Sculptors do use other materials for dummies, but it is hard to make them look as lifelike as they do in wax.

Making figures of historical characters—with no living witnesses left who can testify that the figure looks exactly

15

like the real person—is one thing. But it is quite another to make a wax figure of a person still living who may even have his photograph taken standing next to the mannequin.

This is the challenge that faces the Movieland Wax Museum in California. It was founded by Allen Parkinson, who grew up loving movies and wishing every person in the world could see some of those scenes he enjoyed so much on Saturday afternoons. After a visit to Madame Tussaud's Wax Museum in London, Allen Parkinson suddenly decided that there was a way he could bring back some of the high spots of movies from their earliest days right on up to television films.

But Parkinson realized he would have a problem that never bothers most historical wax museum owners. It would not be enough just to copy pictures carefully. He would have eye-witnesses—many of them very close to the person being done in wax—and each of them would have his own idea how that person really looked. Parkinson had to employ only the most expert wax sculptors, who worked slowly and meticulously. Since each figure costs an average of $2500 and takes almost half a year to complete, the museum grew slowly at first.

The fans vote on the movie, the scene, and the stars they would like most to see in wax. Then the actor or actress poses for three-dimensional photographs and the sculptor takes measurements. No detail is too trivial

The mold made from the clay model turns out a perfect casting in vinyl plastisol

—height, weight, color of complexion, width of shoulders, size of the ears, color of hair and eyes, even the space between the eyes.

While one department works on the scene the dummy is to be starred in, the sculptor begins work on his clay model of the head. He must not leave anything out because so many trifling details go together to make up a whole personality—dimples, moles, wrinkles, veins, muscles, eyebrows, and eyelashes. Just to add the hair to the dummy's head takes 40,000 strands of hair, placed in the wax one at a time. Some sculptors say the mouth and the lines around it are the most important detail to copy. Others say the artist must catch a typical gesture or a characteristic way in which the person stands or tilts his head.

Then there are the little finishing touches. A scene showing Wallace Beery as a bum needs a little dirt added under the fingernails. In "African Queen," Katharine Hepburn's wax face must look shiny and moist from the tropical heat. Bela Lugosi as "Dracula" has a macabre touch of blood on his lips. Even the props must be perfect—a 1933 movie magazine in a scene showing Jean Harlow in a 1933 movie; some rusty, stamped-on tin cans in a scene from "Hondo."

The clothing worn by the dummy stars are often the original clothes from the movie. But when the original cannot be used, the museum makes copies, using the original patterns and materials. Those eyewitnesses have all seen the clothing—probably in wide screen and color close-ups—and they would soon recognize fakes. As "Henry VIII," Charles Laughton wore gold and silk robes. So does his waxen dummy, even though it cost $2500 just to copy the robes. Gloria Swanson donated her $10,000 Russian chinchilla wrap for her wax mannequin to wear. But Brigitte Bardot required the least expensive clothing of all—her dummy wears half a bikini.

Care of the wax dummies in the Movieland Wax Museum is not much different from the care given all wax models. Glass eyes have to be kept polished with a special solution. Occasionally collars need starching or guns need cleaning. Dust is the biggest headache. A gentle feather duster is

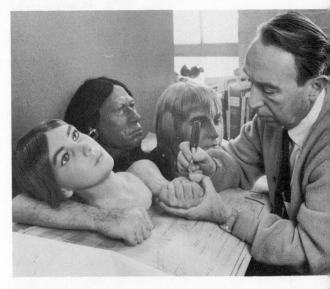

A master sculptor in wax adds the finishing touches

Back at the (wax) ranch, the Cartwrights of Bonanza *fame are ready to start their next TV episode*

17

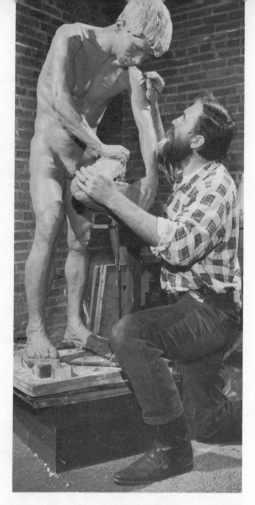

The clay model must display every wrinkle and muscle that will show in the completed wax figure

usually enough, but the "Frankenstein" monster needs a good vacuuming regularly.

Many wax museums now use automation for some of their scenes. There are special effects such as wolves howling and a casket creaking open for "Dracula." "The Absent-minded Professor's" dog barks at museum visitors from his perch in the flying flivver. Edward G. Robinson as "Little Caesar" turns at the sound of a car outside. Suddenly shots are fired and as "Little Caesar" falls forward, the audience sees bullet holes in the glass window. But sometimes the most startling effect can be given just by the imitation of breathing. In Washington, D.C.'s wax museum, Captain John Smith lies helpless, breathing deeply, while Pocahontas pleads for his life. In Hollywood, Vincent Price holds in his arms a lovely lady whom he will add to "The House of Wax" collection just as soon as he drops her into a vat of hot wax, evidently unmoved by the fact that she is still "breathing."

Recently an ad appeared in local newspapers asking for "a man with extra big hands" to apply for a job. The applicants wondered what sort of job it was, but much to their surprise they were not even asked how strong they were or how many dishes they could carry in one armload. The ad meant just what it said, and the man with the biggest hands was chosen. He was ushered with ceremony into the studio of a wax sculptor and his hands were immortalized. Now he can take his family to see the part of him that is famous. His hands are the ones on the wax model of "Frankenstein."

2

Getting to the Heart (and Breath) of the Matter
THE LIFESAVERS

FOR CENTURIES doctors had not been able to figure out how people had died of asphyxia. The word "asphyxia" means "stopping of the pulse," but all the evidence indicated that these people had died because their breathing had stopped. Drowning, being overcome by gas, electric shock, hanging, being buried in a cave-in, a hard blow to the pit of the stomach or back of the neck—all can cause breathing to stop. Even a reaction to drug use stops breathing without warning. To save life, breathing must be started again within a very few minutes.

Until after World War II, the best method of starting a person breathing again was the prone pressure method. All first-aid instructors taught classes of adults and servicemen how to resuscitate victims of asphyxia by forcing the lungs to deflate and inflate as the patient lay face down on the floor. At least the method was easy to learn, and the students could practice on each other, because there was little chance of injuring the student who was

the "victim." Prone pressure methods are still used today if the victim's mouth or nose is damaged badly and also if the rescuer happens not to know any other way of resuscitating. But a new method—with much better results —is preferred by doctors and hospitals.

Actually, mouth-to-mouth and mouth-to-nose resuscitation is not exactly new. An accurate description of how to do it was printed in a best-selling book some five hundred years ago. Unfortunately, the Bible contained many things that people did not understand, although no one questioned them. So when readers came to the part about the way the prophet Elisha revived a little boy about three thousand years ago by breathing air into his mouth, they never dreamed that Elisha was showing them the answer to their centuries-old problem of reviving asphyxiated persons.

Not until 1958 did three doctors convince the world that this "new" method was indeed the best one for adults as well as for infants and children. Approval was vital to keep their

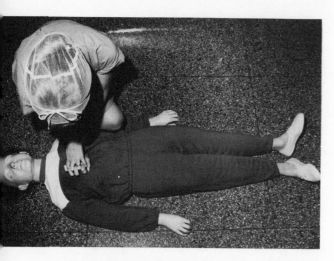

Resusci-Andy obligingly has a coronary for a nurse in training

discovery from getting lost again in the pages of history. But the "new" method did have one problem. How on earth were they ever going to teach it? Everyone who breathes—even a child—is capable of trying to resuscitate a person who has been asphyxiated. But people cannot practice on each other. It would be too dangerous.

Hospitals and industry had all sorts of training manikins. But none was just right for this purpose. Some were too expensive for nonprofessional groups to afford. Some were too heavy. Two hundred pounds of deadweight cannot be tossed into the back seat of a car and driven from one class to another. Some manikins were actually so ugly that would-be rescuers were repulsed just by looking at the body.

When the three doctors met Resusci-Anne, it was love at first sight. She

had been created by Asmund Laerdal, a shy toy and doll maker who was also a book publisher in Stavanger, Norway. The Norwegian Society of Anesthesiologists had asked Laerdal to help them find a way to teach mouth-to-mouth and mouth-to-nose breathing. Making Resusci-Anne had not been too difficult. But when he was ready to shape her face, Laerdal was not satisfied. He had a special feeling about this unusual manikin who was going out into the world to save lives. He didn't want her to look like a lovely movie star or to have a painted face with staring, sightless eyes. He wanted more for Anne—a sort of personality. Then one night, visiting his wife's parents, he found just what he wanted. He was looking at a death mask of a young girl. She had been found drowned in the Seine River in Paris. No one ever found out who she was, but the hint of a smile on her youthful face showed what Laerdal wanted his Anne to have. Anne had never been just a large doll to him— she was special. Now he hoped that the young girl who had drowned would, in a way, live again.

Almost everyone interested in first aid has met Resusci-Anne. She has taught forty million people all over the world—from Boy Scouts to medical students, office workers, and housewives. But she had barely begun her teaching career when a new job was added. Annie needed a "heart."

Just as it is possible for breathing to stop suddenly, it is also possible for the heart to stop. If it is started again without delay, life may continue. But for centuries, no one thought it was possible to start the heart beating again.

One day in 1874, a doctor Moritz Schiff was operating on his dog. He gave it just a little too much chloroform and the dog's heart stopped. Hardly waiting to think, Dr. Schiff cut open his dog's chest and squeezed its heart gently with his fingers while he breathed air into its lungs. The dog revived and was the pride of the entire neighborhood for several years longer. The doctor told many people he knew how he had made the dog's heart start beating again. But he never told anyone in the medical field. It was not until he died in 1896 and his papers were turned over to other doctors that the story became known. His technique, called open chest massage, was used by many doctors until 1960. But using open chest massage with a patient on an operating table was very much different from using it on a man who

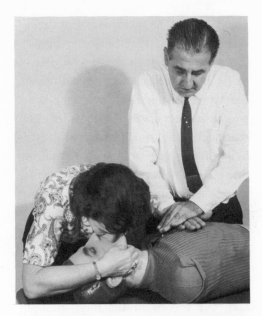

It helps to have two people when mouth-to-mouth resuscitation and external cardiac massage must be done together

ALDERSON RESEARCH LABORATORIES, INC.

drops in the street with a heart attack.

For a man who has a coronary, there should be some way to massage his chest without cutting. Looking back, doctors found many times when the heart had been successfully massaged from outside. But somewhere, the idea had developed that the method worked best on dogs, not people. Next three doctors from Johns Hopkins University School of Medicine perfected external cardiac massage. And it worked best on people. It was not nearly so dangerous as the open chest heart massage. And best of all, it would not be difficult to teach.

That was only because Resusci-Anne was so ready and willing to help —with an empty chest cavity that

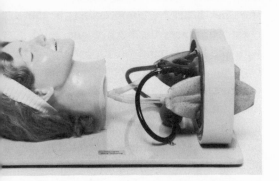

A woman who's easy to see through— that's Anatomic Anne

LAERDAL MEDICAL CORP.

21

could be put to good use. Besides, it often happened that both the breathing and the heart massage would have to be performed at the same time on the same person. Both could be done by the same person if necessary. But that technique was not easy—it was like rubbing the stomach and patting the head at the same time—because the chest is compressed at one rate for breathing but at a different rate for blood circulation. Even teaching this difficult trick was not too much for Resusci-Anne.

Resusci-Anne has bag will travel. In fact, she travels in the bag, all doubled over with a bottle of spray disinfectant, some plastic sheeting to use for face masks, a pump to blow her up, some glue and patches for repairs, and a gauge to show how well her pupils are learning. Her assistant places her on a firm surface, puts her heart and lungs in place, then inflates her. As soon as he places a clear, plastic mask over her face, to keep trainees from trading germs with each other, he punctures holes where the mouth and nostrils are. Now Anne is ready to start teaching.

Anne's lifelike qualities are very important to the trainee. She comes in a Negro, as well as an Oriental, version for more realism. And realism is important. If the would-be rescuer feels he is only playing with an overgrown doll, he may not be able to act when he finds himself in a real emergency with a real person.

The trainee tilts back Anne's head to clear the air passages. Her lungs won't inflate any more than a human's would unless her head is tilted properly. Pinching the nostrils closed and breathing deeply into Anne's mouth—about fifteen times a minute—the trainee removes his mouth from hers to glance at her chest. It should rise and fall normally. Only Anne's helper can watch the gauge to see whether the trainee is breathing too deeply, too lightly, or just right. After all, humans do not have gauges, so the rescuer must learn to resuscitate by watching his patient's life signs. Mouth-to-nose resuscitation is done the same way, except that the trainee gently closes Anne's mouth while forcing air into her nostrils. The trainee's mouth must make a tight seal over whichever place the air is forced in.

After the trainee has learned to start Anne breathing, he is ready for the next step. He locates the carotid artery in her neck. If he cannot feel or see a pulse in the carotid artery, chances are that Anne is suffering from heart arrest. The rescuer must start her heart by compression on the chest. He places the heel of one hand, with the other hand on top of it, just over the lower third of the sternum, or breastbone. He pushes down about once every second to force the heart against the spine. The compression pumps blood from the heart into the arteries and from the veins into the heart. But this would not be safe to practice on anyone except Resusci-Anne. A well person's ribs could be broken by the compression. But the rib cage of a person with heart arrest is more flexible than that of a well person. For that reason, the rescuer can push down hard an inch and a half to two inches to compress the heart. Anne's body is made to react in the same way as the body of a person whose heart has stopped—not like the body of the well person.

The real test for a rescuer comes when he must give both cardiac massage and resuscitation at the same time. Two people can do the two jobs together, although each has a different rhythm. But accidents hardly ever happen conveniently, so the trainee must learn to do both jobs himself—a good illustration of perpetual motion. There should be five heart compressions for every breath!

After training class, Anne is deflated and flipped back into her suitcase. The disinfectant is sprayed into her mouth and nostrils. Now she is ready for the next class.

Anne turned out to be so much in demand in the world of lifesaving it is not surprising that she could not do all the jobs. A rescue crew training to save miners from asphyxiation in cave-ins, for example, would hardly expect to find a lady in the mines. So Resusci-Andy is available for occasions when a boy manikin is preferred.

When instructors found that some of their trainees could not understand what happens inside Anne when she is given heart massage or resuscitation, they thought of a see-through model.

Anatomic Anne was born. Now the trainee could actually see how the lungs inflate or how compression forces blood to move through the heart.

Suddenly a hospital nurse in charge of the newborn babies notices that one of the infants is turning blue. His tiny lungs are not used to breathing, and have stopped. This is no spot for an amateur to find herself in. Fortunately every nurse in this infant nursery has met someone like Resusci-Baby.

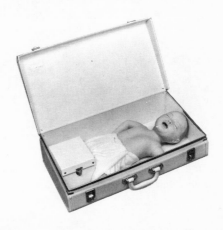

Between resuscitation classes, Resusci-Baby lives in a suitcase

LAERDAL MEDICAL CORP.

Quickly she clears the baby's air passages and bends over to breathe carefully into his tiny lungs. Twenty to thirty small puffs of air a minute from her cheeks is enough. If the infant's heart should stop beating, only two fingertips are used to depress his sternum a hundred times a minute.

Another model of Resusci-Baby has a perfectly modeled mouth and tra-

23

chea. There are many emergencies when a doctor must put a tube down an infant's throat. But just as the nurse had to practice on someone, so does the doctor. Resusci-Baby gives both of them a good chance to learn how to put the breathing tube in a tiny baby.

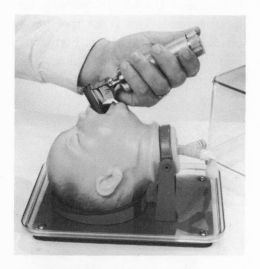

Placing a tube in a baby's tiny trachea is a technique that takes practice
LAERDAL MEDICAL CORP.

Arrhythmia Anne has a heart, but her heart is not a healthy one. It is electronically controlled by the instructor so that medical students can learn to recognize at a glance any one of eight different heart disorders. A doctor must be able to make the right decision in every heart case, because often he will not have a chance to make another choice. Only years of experience with heart patients can give him all the training he really needs. The problem is that a beginning doctor rarely gets to see the "interesting" pa-

tients. He has to learn from hearing older doctors tell about their special patients or by listening endlessly to records playing the sounds of irregular heartbeats.

Arrhythmia Anne can help medical students as well as doctors by imitating all the symptoms of the most common heart ailments. The student holds electrodes as the instructor decides what symptoms he will have Arrhythmia Anne show. By placing the electrodes properly the student can shock her heart back into a normal state. Or the instructor may add more problems to her original heart disorder, giving the medical student a real workout. When all his efforts fail to start the heart beating normally, he may still "save" his patient with external cardiac massage. A real-life chain of events—such as a student might never see—is available thanks to Arrhythmia Anne.

An entirely different line of work is taken up by the manikin, Rescutrain. He has a talent for getting himself into the most tense situations. Since his size (5'9") and weight (180 pounds) are those of the average man, he volunteers for some of the nastiest jobs around.

Dressed in coveralls—with work gloves for hands and foam-filled work shoes for feet—he reports for the day's work. First thing, an inexperienced lineman has touched the wrong wire at the top of an electric pole. Sure enough, it's that problem character, Rescutrain! Bill, a new lineman is below, waiting to dash to the rescue as soon as fellow crewmen turn off the electric current. Quickly Bill clambers up the pole, reaching Rescutrain actually only a few seconds after the accident. There is no carotid pulse and there is not a second to waste—not even time to call down below and tell the others what is wrong. Bill immediately begins mouth-to-mouth resuscitation and external cardiac massage. There is no room at the top of the pole for a helper, so Bill must do both jobs himself. He struggles to remember the technique he learned on the manikin in class. Was it five compression strokes to one breath? Or the other way around? Fortunately Bill remembers and Rescutrain is revived.

Many electric and telephone company linemen owe their lives to the new technique of resuscitation and heart massage. Until a dummy came to the rescue, valuable time was wasted because the injured man had to be lowered to the ground so he could be laid flat for the prone pressure method of artificial respiration. The new type can be performed at the top of the pole.

Rescutrain has a sling attached to his back to help hoist him into the impossible situations dreamed up for the trainee to rescue him from. His weight is distributed much the same as a real man's. His head tilts backward and also turns like a human's. Even his legs, hips, and knees flex so he can be placed in realistic positions. The trainee knows he is resuscitating properly when he sees Rescutrain's chest

After pole-top resuscitation, Rescutrain is gently lowered to the ground
ALDERSON RESEARCH LABORATORIES, INC.

rise and fall naturally. Gauges in his shoulders show when the lungs receive ventilation or the heart gets enough pressure, but the gauges are for the instructor to read. The trainee watches the life signs to see how Rescutrain is doing.

Rescutrain's next job may be showing novice window washers how the safety belt would catch them in case they slip. Or he might test a parachute. Perhaps he is to be rescued from a burning building. A fireman trainee lowers him from a window to the ground. Another trainee practices lowering him from the window to a ladder where a fireman is waiting to start resuscitation at the top of the ladder. Later Rescutrain may play the starring role in a cave-in accident and have to be resuscitated while other rescue workers learn how to dig him free without causing more cave-in. For a switch in the afternoon's program, Rescutrain is an auto-crash victim. While trainees use a blowtorch to free him from behind the wheel of a crushed auto, other trainees give him heart massage and resuscitation.

Each dummy has his own particular field. While Rescutrain is often saved from burning buildings, he is there only to be rescued. How badly, some people wonder, might he have been burned? For this study another dummy is needed. A transparent manikin, the size of an average person, is a new invention by a Russian medical team. His transparent surface is divided into a number of equal areas separated by opaque walls. Through the use of light shining into those areas known to have received burn damage, doctors can measure how much more of the area around the severe burns has also been affected. The knowledge can be used in treating the burns as well as in designing clothing that would have protected the body better.

Although Congress has not yet voted a medal for the unselfish lifesaving manikin, dummies are beginning to be appreciated for their lifetime of devotion to mankind.

3

The Mod, Mad, Dummy World

MODELS OF FASHION

A T 2:30 A.M. the burglar alarm sounded. Police cars pulled up outside a large Philadelphia department store. Security guards at the store said the burglar alarm had been tripped by someone inside. And since the doors were still locked, he must still be in there. Guards and police prowled through the store's aisles. The guards stationed at the door kept insisting no one had gone out past them. But there was no burglar to be found.

Finally the police called in the Canine Corps. The trained dogs sniffed excitedly up and down the aisles, bumping into mannequins. The search had gone on about four hours when one of the security guards stopped to rest against a handbag counter. Glancing up at a figure on the glass counter, he remarked aloud how lifelike store dummies are today. This one was a little too lifelike. He burst out laughing and was arrested on the spot. "Hiding" in full view of the searchers had been easy for Herman, a juvenile burglar, because the store employs about fifty dummies. They all looked as real as

Herman, but they are a little smarter.

A fashion dummy has to be smart to hold a job today. Almost every year the "ideal" figure changes. One year a flat tummy look is in; the next year a flat backside is more fashionable. But it was not always that way. Fashionable ladies padded their clothing from underneath so they could stick out wherever they wished. The problem began when women's dummies were liberated from the attic to the fashion window.

For centuries women made clothes at home—their own as well as their children's and husbands' everyday clothing. Wealthier families could afford to go to a dressmaker for the party clothes. But everyday clothes were fairly simple and formfitting. There were no patterns at all. Clothes were made by the trial and error method. The least twitchy member of the family was usually drafted to stand on a table to be the "body" and hold up the fabric while it was pinned, cut, draped, pinned again, and cut some more.

When queens as long ago as the four-

An early department store dummy with no hair problem—it wore plaster

teenth century wanted something special to wear, however, they sent for a fashion doll to see what was being worn in the best circles of Paris. Fashion dolls were generally one third to one half human size, but the queen-size mannequins were exactly the measurements of their prospective royal customers. This was special service so that the queens could try the clothes on themselves as well.

France was not always on the best of terms with other countries. While ambassadors floundered in protocol and foreign languages, there were many occasions when a mannequin—dressed in the latest Parisian styles—did the "talking" instead. In 1396, the court tailor of Charles VI turned in his bill for 450 francs to pay for the wardrobe he had made for a doll—a gift to the English queen from the Bavarian queen. Another French king, Henri IV, sent mannequins to do his wooing for him. Wise to his intended bride's love of fashionable clothes and knowing his own inability to say the right words at the right time, he sent several fashion dolls to show Marie de' Medici "a sample of our fashions." The mannequins did the trick and the lady quickly said "Yes."

During the reign of Louis XIV, fashions changed so often—sleeve styles changed nine times in one year—that dolls bounced back and forth regularly between countries in spite of four major wars that kept people from crossing borders safely. In 1704, during the war of the Spanish Succession, prime ministers on both sides of the battle lines granted special passes so the mannequins could travel. "By an act of gallantry which is worthy of being noted in the chronicles of history for the benefit of the ladies," wrote the Abbé Prévost, "that pass was always respected, and during the times of greatest enmity experienced on both sides, the mannequin was the one object which remained unmolested."

Meanwhile, the New World was being supplied with fashion dolls sent from England. "Waiting for the ship to come in" may have meant commerce and money in the pocket to the men in the colonies, but to the women who could afford them, it meant new fashions. As soon as the ship docked, the *New England Weekly Journal* or some other newspaper would adver-

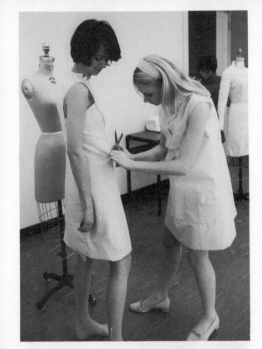

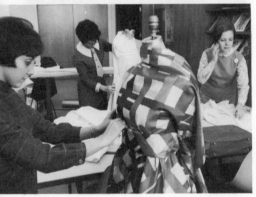

Dressmaking students fit muslin patterns on each other, while dummies stand ready

A dummy can stand still indefinitely and doesn't mind being stuck with pins
DREXEL UNIVERSITY, PHILADELPHIA

tize that "a mannequin in the latest fashion . . . with articles of dress, night-dresses and everything pertaining to woman's attire" could now be seen at the shop of a local dressmaker. In the same newspapers, fashion editors described down to the last velvet ribbon exactly what clothes were now being worn by fashionable European women.

Dresses were becoming so hard to make that many fathers despaired that their daughters were running them to the poorhouse. Their mothers—or at least their dressmakers—despaired too. There were still no dress patterns, and an unskilled dressmaker could waste a lot of material trying to copy a dress without a pattern to guide her. As dress styles changed to close-fitting garments, someone invented the dressmaker's dummy.

The earliest dummies for home use were woven of reeds. They were lightweight, but easily broken. Wax dummies were more attractive, but could not be stored in a hot attic for fear of melting. The perfect dressmaker's dummy a century ago seemed to be the one made of a new product—rubber. It could be blown up enough to model for the fat housewife or the air could be let out so it became a model for skinny Aunt Matilda. Unfortunately, pins and needles cut short the rubber dummy's career with a bang. Papier-mâché had been used for just about everything made in the home in the late 1800's, so it was understandable that someone would try it for dummies too. The lady who needed a dressmaker's dummy could get together the necessary materials for papier-mâché-making and invite a close friend or two in for the afternoon. Then putting on a simple thin undergarment, she allowed herself to be wrapped round and round with strips of the papier-mâché material. When it was dry and hard, the form was slit carefully up the side and the lady stepped out free. Fastened together again and shellacked for protection, the dummy was now an exact copy of the lady's figure—at least until she grew fatter or thinner.

Eventually mechanical forms came along, with the torso divided into segments. By turning a screw here and there, the hips could be made to grow fatter or the waist thinner so one dummy could be used by all the women in a family. Any odd shape the dummy could not duplicate was made by adding corsets, bustles, waist cinchers, and crinolines that bent the person instead of the dummy into the desired shape.

A big day in the life of a fashionable family in the late 1800's was the day scheduled for the arrival of the visiting seamstress. In those days a person could not just drive into the city to buy a shirt or dress. She went to a dry goods store and selected the material. Then the housewife took it home to make what she needed. If the store was one of the new large dry goods stores in a city, she might have the choice of selecting the material and sending it upstairs to have one of the store's hundred seamstresses on the upper floors make it for her. But most families were large and for them it was more convenient and cheaper to have the seamstress come and live in for a week or so. The dummy was brought out of the attic and set up in the "sew-

Two mannequins that draw in different types of customers

ing room" that would be the seamstress' own domain. There she would sleep, work, and sometimes even eat.

It was like having an old friend visit when the seamstress came. Many unmarried ladies who were clever with the needle earned their living by moving from family to family. Usually the seamstress returned year after year to the same home where she watched the children grow from crib to college dressed in the clothing she made. In a few weeks' time, she could outfit a mother, four daughters, and four sons in enough apparel (and local gossip) to last until her next visit. Often she made shirts and underclothes for the father of the house too. She made night-

30

gowns, petticoats, chemises, and underpants—all edged in Irish lace with pale pink and blue ribbons threaded through the lace. She made sailor suits for little boys and velvet suits with Little Lord Fauntleroy collars. She could balance the latest *Godey's Lady's Book* open at the fashion page on one knee while she pin fitted the material on the dummy in an exact imitation of the dress someone wanted. She was also good at whittling down big sister's best party dress to fit sister number two this year and sister number three next year.

The floor of the sewing room was littered with pins and scraps of material because the seamstress never stopped working long enough to clean up. And always in the corner stood the dressmaker's dummy—rarely seen without its white sheet covering, because there

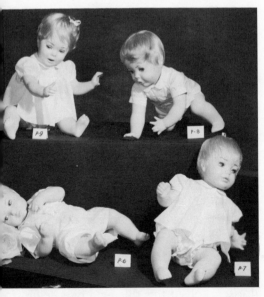

Some of the younger specialists holding jobs in department stores

was something faintly indecent about a human torso. When the sewing was finished at last, the seamstress packed up her scissors and pins and moved on to the next customer's house. The dummy was hustled back up to the attic. Dummies were not ready yet to appear in public.

While the West was still coping with a few Indian uprisings, some of the large Eastern cities were experimenting with a strange new idea—the "department" store. Until now, a city shopper who wanted to make a dress had to go to many different stores to collect her sewing needs. Often she had to traipse all over town collecting fabric, buttons, thread, needles and pins, whalebone stays, lace and ribbon, hooks and eyes, stiffening, and scissors. Finally someone thought of putting all those necessary items in the same store! It was a most unusual idea, but the ladies really went for it. Oddly enough, it was another fifty years before store managers could move their "dry goods" from the first floor of the store up to a higher floor. Even after ready-made dresses and suits arrived in stores, it was unthinkable not to display the dress materials where they could be seen the second the customer set foot in the store. The old dressmaker's dummy played a small part in this revolutionary change.

Outside the store, there was a window—sometimes. Later, stores would be designed with large show windows, but at first a sign reading DRY GOODS was thought to be advertisement

31

enough. The customers would see the dry goods as soon as they came in. Who needed a window to show their wares in?

Store owners soon found out who needed a window—as soon as the competition got stiffer. Prospective customers were passing by on the sidewalk outside all day long. A store manager, observing from his second-floor office, would see people stop at a store across the street. They might linger at a window, then turn in at the door. To all appearances those people had simply been walking past. They had not planned to go in a store to buy. But something in the store window had created the desire to buy and presto! the passerby had turned like magic into a buying customer.

The first window trimmers crammed everything they could find into the show windows. "The more items we have in our windows, the more the customer will think he can find in our store," said the managers confidently. But that is not the way it worked. There was so much showing that a customer could not find what he was looking for, even when he knew it was there. So window trimming became "window decorating"—a much more sophisticated art. Merchants tried to outdo each other by attracting attention with more and more exotic ornaments. An unusual dress might attract the women, but a dress looked limp and undesirable hung on the wall or draped on the floor. In the early 1900's a few window decorators were bold

Things don't always go right—even for a dummy

DECTER MANNIKIN CO., INC.

enough to bring the old dressmaker's dummy out of the attic and slip a dress on it. The dress looked better, but the first window dummies had no heads or arms and had a stand instead of feet. Even in New York City, where everything new is tried, dummies had no heads until 1914.

After dummies had made their timid appearance in public windows and store owners found their customers were not offended to see a dressed torso, they got braver and used a few of the new plaster models that had been created by a sculptor. These turned out to be extremely heavy and almost impossible to dress. Window dressers solved this dilemma by sawing the plaster models in half. They could now be carried easily and dressed in store. Their daintily crooked fingers and haughty stances simply did not say "Come on inside" to the lookers. Window trimmers racked their brains for something that would "catch the customer's eye." Some of the furniture and props in Marshall Field's windows in Chicago were so elegant that they were bought up by a local art institute. But the sad fact seemed to be that a dummy with a bucket of sand at her feet seemed to be selling beach clothing

Teen-age mannequins look swinging even when sitting still

DECTER MANNIKIN CO., INC.

half the time. They were expensive and easily chipped, but even a dummy with a fractured ear and chipped nose seemed to be doing a good job of selling clothes. Venturing a little farther, storekeepers tried dummies with real hair. A hairdresser was busy almost every day arranging and curling these expensive heads with her electric curling iron and bobby pins.

But something was missing, and it took a depression to show store owners what it was. The window dummies all had simpering little spoiled-debutante faces that stared blindly out the window over the heads of the ordinary customers. Few window shoppers identified themselves with these tall, obviously wealthy dummies who wore the most exclusive clothing sold in the

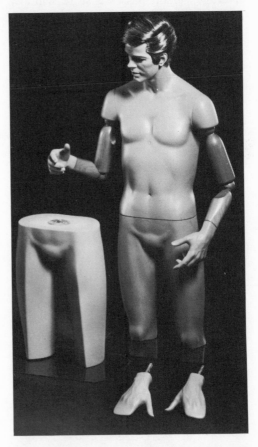

Legs that keep a trouser crease, jointed flex arms, and flat hands to use in pockets, are all part of a male mannequin's gear

DECTER MANNIKIN CO., INC.

33

better than one standing beside a hideously expensive model of the Taj Mahal!

The depression of 1929 was disastrous to many people, but it was a blessing in disguise to the mannequin world. Large stores could no longer spend great sums of money to make their windows outstanding. The window decorators would have to get a whole new set of ideas for attracting attention. Someone figured out that the average person passes a store window in about eleven seconds. In that length of time, a mannequin had to make a customer forget where she had intended to go and turn into the store to buy something she had no intention of buying! This was no easy job for a dummy—especially now that people had less money than ever. Yet, the store manager worried, people had to have clothes. How could they be made to buy? It did not take him too long to realize that his dummies—at least the ones he had then—were simply not up to the job expected of them. Their arrogant looks were turning people off. Besides, the expensive cruise clothing and dinner-at-the-country-club formal

 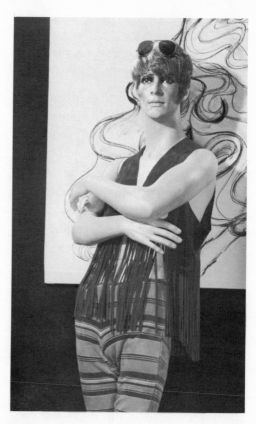

In ten years, the male image changed in mannequins as it did in people

gowns were not what people wanted to see, now that business was bad for everyone.

So, in the beginning of the depression, dummies suddenly became friendly-looking. Their faces wore companionable, gamin expressions. They dressed in sports clothes, raincoats, office dresses, and suits. Their hands stopped looking as if they were made to hold a teacup and looked more like hands that might hold a broom or handbag. Their hair stopped looking as if it required the services of a hairdresser once a week to keep it looking right. One final touch was needed to bring the window shopper into the store—the price tags were showing. Now the shopper looking for a dress was not put in the embarrassing position of asking the price inside. Before she entered, she learned, from the mannequins in the window, whether she had enough money in her purse. In spite of hard times, store owners began to breathe deeply again. The crisis was over. Clothes began to sell.

Once mannequins had proved how well they could sell, every store wanted some inside, as well as outside. But they were still expensive and easily damaged. A plaster dummy cost up to $150 in 1937 and even then it lasted only a few years. Wax dummies cost twice as much. Some stores bought "woodikins," made in Germany, for only $25. But they were flat across the back and clothes had to be pinned on them crudely.

Today about fifty to seventy-five

Abstract torsos have changeable pedestals and tops (called caps) for modeling pants, skirts, dresses, blouses
DECTER MANNIKIN CO., INC.

mannequins have full-time jobs in a large department store, with fifty more waiting in the storerooms. Mannequins have their "specialists" just as any professional group does. A lying-down mannequin can do nothing but lie down. She is handy to have if a store sells lingerie, but not so good if the store specializes in sportswear or suits to wear to the office. A model with her hands on her hips is doomed to go through her life in that position. Some have their faces modeled after famous people—Barbra Streisand, Audrey Hepburn, Naomi Sims, Grace Kelly. But they are copies only from the neck up—the bodies are made to fit certain dress sizes. In addition, they also are limited in what they can do. It would be ridiculous for the Princess of Monaco to model housedresses or Barbra

35

Streisand to appear in blue jeans. They work only in the main street windows. Less important faces are usually sent to the side street windows. Most dummies that look vaguely familiar are copied from real models or socialites who appear in fashion magazines. Their names are never revealed.

Just as many industries have testing grounds, so has a department store. They are called boutiques. Most have specially designed mannequins that show off the newest mod styles sold in the boutique. A boutique for the teen-age crowd usually has the kind of music playing that tells older folks instinctively that they will not find their sort of clothes there. Sometimes a soft drink bar is set up to pull in the pre-teen group. Mannequins chosen to work in these specialty shops are designed to fit in with their unique surroundings. They may follow one of the new abstract images or even be made of chicken wire.

When the display manager plans the city store's window displays for the season, he has many decisions to make. If he shows sporty clothes, he chooses mannequins that show action and are bubbling over with good health. Romantic or exotic clothing can be shown on a pale dummy in a relaxed pose. There are various interchangeable pieces the displayer can use. A male model standing with his hands in his pockets rumples up his neat suit unless a flat hand made especially to slip into pockets without causing wrinkles is substituted for his regular hand. One manufacturer makes legs for male dummies that are in the shape of creased pants so there is no danger of his trousers looking baggy before the next window change. Lady dummies have changeable hands also so they can make gestures or hold a matching handbag properly. Rubber hands are made for ladies wearing gloves. Toes on the feet are usually stuck together, because putting shoes on mannequins is the hardest job of all. But when a model wears toeless sandals, she must wear feet with separated toes. When a lady wears a hat, she cannot wear an ordinary wig or her hat will perch up on top like a clown's. She is fitted instead with a "cap wig"—something that many humans who try to wear wigs under their hats should know about. A lady dummy has dozens of wigs to choose from so that when modeling a bathing suit, she doesn't need to look as if her hair was done for a night at the opera.

The display crew also decides whether to use some of the personable new Negro models. Since the first Negro mannequin appeared in 1964, department stores all over the United States have added them to their shopping list. Now they come in all ages and sizes, male and female. The important point is that they are not simply darkened versions of the old white mannequins. They have attractive racial features and hair styles. Oriental models are popular too, especially in cities with a large Oriental population. Until the last few years, most of the

Just like people—mannequins have different racial backgrounds

mannequins in Tokyo windows looked like Americans instead of Orientals.

For every customer who likes to see a mannequin that looks very human, there is another who says mannequins distract from the clothing they are trying to sell. So rather than lose their jobs entirely, some dummies have gone over to the abstract or stylized form. This can be carried to extremes,

though, like the department store that displays a tee shirt on a T-shaped piece of sewer pipe.

Once the decisions are made on who goes into the windows and what they will wear, the props are collected and the window display crew faces a long night. Although the depression of 1929 is long past, store windows never returned to the lavish and extravagant displays that characterized earlier windows. Props are subtle and suggestive instead. No matter how successful a window display is, it will never be repeated. The props may be kept, but if they are used again, they will look entirely different.

The newest mannequins have bulletproof skin—not because they might be shot at, but because they need to be made of the same tough material used to make bulletproof vests. These dummies come apart much more easily than their ancestors. A mannequin that wears slacks has one leg that unscrews, but the other is not removable. Most now come apart at the hips rather than at the waist—a change brought about by bikini bathing suits and hiphugger pants. A slash across the waistline just did not look right. The hands come off for easy sleeve-pulling, but the division is a little above the wrist line so it is not noticeable. Both arms remove at the shoulder. Men's mannequins sometimes have flexible arms with joints that are hidden in the jacket so they can be positioned naturally.

An experienced dresser can clothe a mannequin completely in about a

37

half hour. The human foot is extremely flexible. But shoes are a problem for the dresser. Shoes made for a human balk when it comes to stiff mannequin feet.

Recently a New York store that carries hiphuggers and the sort of expensive men's clothing worn by the wealthy man of action found that none of its mannequins looked right in up-to-the-minute sports clothes. Its 1965 crewcut dummy might have looked fine in a gray flannel businessman's suit, but he looked like an impostor in clothes for the next decade. Nor could any of the handsome dummies lined up in the storeroom do the job. A more masculine type was needed— and one that was definitely "not pretty." A removable wig and mustache, in case hair styles changed drastically, would be good too. Finally the store located a man it thought looked just right and put a sculptor to work copying his face. The result is a new dummy that looks startlingly real, his Riviera suntan and rippling muscles attracting as much attention as his outfits.

4

Dummies for the Birds (and Beasts)

ANIMAL DUMMIES

THERE WAS A WAR on in the colonies, but English people who wanted to forget could spend an afternoon at Sir Ashton Lever's. Sir Ashton had begun by collecting live birds, but when some of the favorites died, he had them stuffed. And from there, his museum grew to be like many others—overridden with unclassified shells and fossils, savage weapons, costumes, and stuffed animals. Still, in its way, his museum was unusual, and Sir Ashton aimed to keep it spectacular.

In Sir Ashton's stuffy manner this meant not only charging admission but being very choosy about his museum's visitors. In September, 1773, he placed an ad in the London newspapers that laid it right on the line. He informed the public that "being tired out with the insolence of the common People, who I have hitherto indulged with a sight of my museum, . . . I am now come to the resolution of refusing admittance to the lower class except they come provided with a ticket from some Gentleman or Lady of my acquaintance." Even then, the "common People" were

not to be allowed in the museum during the same hours that ladies and gentlemen were there. No reason was given for keeping certain people out, unless it was that they could not keep from bursting out laughing at the sight of the museum's director, Sir Ashton, cavorting through the shrubbery dressed in Robin Hood greens, shooting bows and arrows into the underbrush.

This tendency to "entertain" museum visitors, rather than to educate them, was one of the big problems of all early museums. Since most of the treasures were kept in cabinets, they were not the most exciting places to spend an afternoon. Many museum owners tried to add unusual touches to draw the crowds. Some kept on hand a few live animals, wax figures of kings and South Sea islanders, or curiosities that ranged from gallstones (contributed by the doctor who had removed them from a patient) to hair balls (taken from the stomachs of animals that licked their long hair). One of the best museums in the New World

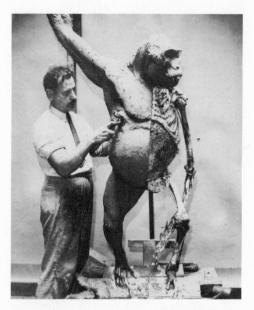

After this gorilla's skeleton is rebuilt, he is given a "skin" of clay

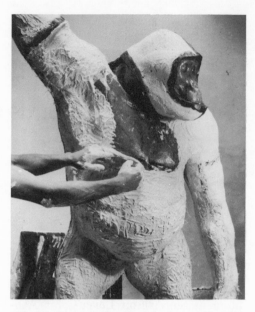

The shellacked clay is covered over with plaster to make a mold

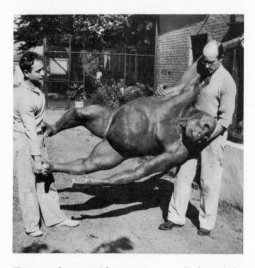

From the mold comes a lightweight papier-mâché gorilla

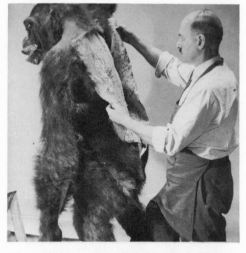

The gorilla is glued back into his skin

was owned by Charles Willson Peale in Philadelphia, who was fortunate enough to have unearthed the skeleton of a mastodon to draw his crowds.

Peale had a real feeling for natural history and was a masterful taxidermist besides. But he was not without problems. His prize exhibits were kept

It's now ready for its new "jungle" home

locked in glass cases, not so much to keep people out as to keep insects from getting in. Rats and mice took their toll of the stuffed animals on display, but moths brought the biggest headaches. Peale tried dipping his smaller animals in turpentine and then experimented with different kinds of stuffing material. But it was no use. Finally he brewed a huge kettle of arsenic solution and dipped his specimens into it, nearly killing himself with arsenic poisoning in the process.

Peale was also an artist and a sculptor, and when he mounted a natural history specimen, he put all his talents to work at once. After making a wooden sculpture of the animal that was "accurate enough to show the play of the muscles," as Peale put it, he stretched the skin tightly over the model. On those days he was thankful for the years of experience he had spent as apprentice to a saddlemaker. He was proud that his animals were better than just "stuffed" animals.

41

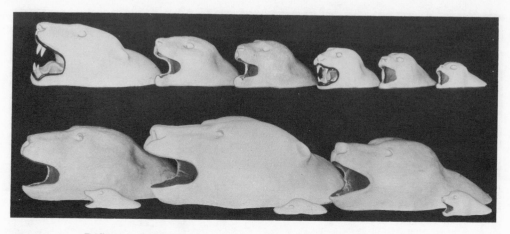

Different size heads waiting for rugs to fit them

The artist in Peale and in his sons came out when they tried to display their animals by showing a little of the natural habitat. Peale made an artificial pond for ducks and a tree to hold birds—some in the act of landing with wings outstretched, some preening their feathers, some on nests. Most taxidermists found it easiest to keep their animals' mouths shut. But not Peale. He said the teeth showed the character of the species, and he often showed animals snarling or howling. Unfortunately for Peale, the time had not yet come when people were interested enough in museums to help support them. More space cost money and unless there was space, the museum Peale dreamed of could never come true.

A hundred years later, Carl Akeley, a noted explorer, came back from Africa with some very unusual specimens and an even more unusual idea. He was a taxidermist and knew that the old methods of stuffing animals and preserving skins would not work with the animals he planned to bring home. Akeley skinned his animals in the field as soon as they were killed. With a few deft slits, an animal's fur coat can be removed as easily as stripping off a pair of long underwear. A plaster mold was immediately made of the carcass before the vultures settled down to make a dinner of it. The fur—or skin—was salted and packed away for the long trip home by ship, and the plaster cast was also packed carefully. Back at the museum, the plaster mold was used to make a model of the animal. When the fur had been treated to prevent moth damage, it was stretched over the dummy that had been made from the animal's carcass. Of course it fit perfectly.

Today, natural history museums still use Akeley's method of skinning the animal in the field. With large animals, the bones too are shipped. Thanks to air travel, the chances of

The finished mount of a sheep

JONAS BROS., INC., DENVER

losing any skins from rotting are gone. Beetles are used to clean off the bones, but new research has turned up bacterial cultures controlled by enzymes that can do in forty-eight hours what it takes beetles six weeks to do.

The animal is rebuilt in skeleton form first. Then a wire mesh covers the bone armature and papier-mâché may be used to fill in awkward hollow places. The taxidermist has before him sketches of this particular animal made in the field and a complete set of anatomical measurements and photographs made immediately after the animal was killed. He also has sketches showing him the position this particular dummy will stand in the finished exhibit.

He covers over the wire and bone skeleton with clay. On this clay will be sculpted every single wrinkle and bulge that is to show on the completed dummy. After the clay dries, it is shellacked. The figure has become very heavy and cumbersome. Now a plaster mold is made of the clay model. The plaster is mixed with tow—the coarse part of hemp—and so it is much tougher than the old plaster molds that

Akeley used to make over the animal's carcass. After the plaster mold is removed from the clay model, the animal is stripped back down to the bare bones again. His bones are put away in a "skeleton bank" to be used again sometime.

The plaster mold is used to model a strong, lightweight manikin from papier-mâché or from a new lightweight plastic. A metal rod inside helps to strengthen the dummy, but this model is hollow and easy to move around. Next the eyes are attached and some plastic teeth if the animal's own were no good. At last, the bare dummy is ready for his fur or skin coat, which by now has been through a tanning process and is as soft as a lady's fur coat. After the skin is cemented onto the dummy, the job is done.

A small animal—less than the size

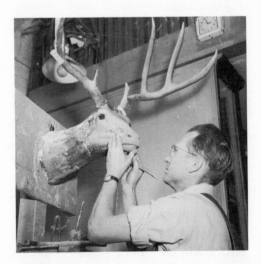

Antlers, eyes, lips, and nostrils are all ready before the hide is slipped on and glued.

JONAS BROS., INC., DENVER, and DENVER POST

43

of a fox—can be freeze-dried just as it is, so that no skinning or mounting needs to be done. It must be placed in position exactly as wanted immediately after being killed and before it has a chance to stiffen. The animal is frozen solid very quickly and then placed in a vacuum tank for several weeks to remove every last drop of moisture in the body. The body doesn't "melt," but the ice crystals are changed directly to vapor. Once a freeze-dried specimen has been taken from the vacuum tank, it will last indefinitely at room temperature. But such animals cannot really be called "dummies," since they are still the real thing.

One taxidermy company makes small animal dummies using a new flexible plastic material. The flexiforms make it much simpler to construct the small, hard-to-work-with dummies and have certain advantages over the long freeze-dried process.

Birds are also "skinned out" in the field and shipped to the taxidermist packed in dry ice. There the skin is put over forms that can be made of anything, such as balsa wood, styrofoam, or papier-mâché, and wires are put in to strengthen the legs, wings, and neck. The skin is sewed back on with dental floss.

The taxidermist has shelves of supplies to make animal dummies look natural. He has artificial eyes of every size from the tiniest snake's to the giraffe's. He has yellow eyes with black centers for a pelican; speckled brown with a vertical slit pupil for an alligator; brown with a purple horizontal slit pupil for a mountain goat or buffalo; or a motley red with an oval red pupil for an albino deer. His shelves of artificial teeth show the jaws of almost any animal—and next to them are the tongues. He has ear liners, half heads to make animal rugs, ready-made forms for every kind of animal, even artificial rocks for animals to stand on. But unless the hunter does his part of the job, the taxidermist cannot turn out a good animal.

The hunter must fulfill two conditions if he expects to have a good-looking trophy in his den. First he has to catch one. All animals have an instinctive fear. All animals also have some unique equipment for avoiding the trophy room.

Bears are dangerous and very likely to charge the hunter, especially when they are hungry and angered at being disturbed in their search for food. Unfortunately, the time to get a bear is in spring when he is easiest to find and his fur is at its thickest—and when he is also at his hungriest. Rocky Mountain goats are not too dangerous, but the ground they inhabit is. While they have concave-shaped hooves that act like suction cups when pressed down, the hunter has no such accesories. Even if he does manage to get close enough to aim at a mountain goat and hit it, the wounded goat often pulls himself to the edge of a cliff. The hunter's prized trophy smashes down a few thousand feet of solid rock and there is nothing left to take home.

While an elephant may have poor eyesight, he makes up for it with his senses of smell and hearing and his aggressive nature when he is disturbed. The lion has excellent eyes, but is extremely cunning about hiding himself when he is wounded and can lead the hunter through miles of dangerous country. Having wounded a lion, the hunter is bound by the rules of the hunt to follow it. If he does not, the wounded lion could turn into a man-killer.

If the hunter finally succeeds in landing himself a trophy, his conditions are only half met. He must now immediately remove the skin and prepare it for the trip to the taxidermist. There is barely time to have his photograph taken beside the dead animal and to take the measurements of his kill, which are especially important if he wants a full life-size dummy made.

Skinning the animal is not difficult and takes no more than a good hunting or skinning knife, but it cannot be left until tomorrow, no matter how tired the hunter is. Every part of the animal's fur or hide must be skinned out. There are many little tricks, such as leaving the pads on the bottom of the feet and the claws on if it is to be a full figure. Skinning the skull is the hardest, because the ears, eyelids, and lips take special care. An animal with antlers or horns is skinned completely, then the top of the skull is sawed off and removed with the horns.

Most inexperienced hunters have trouble when it comes to salting and drying out the hides. All the extra flesh and fat must be taken off or the salt won't get down into the pores. The salt is rubbed hard into every portion. Where skin is wrinkled, it must be straightened out and salted. Any tiny section that is not salted will rot. After salting, the skin is rolled up and left a few hours. Later, it can be opened out and aired in a shady place until almost dry, but never put in the sun or near a fire. When the skin is finally ready to send to the taxidermist, it will be rolled up with the fur side inside.

Now it is the taxidermist's turn to do his part. Probably before the hunter even left home, he knew what sort of animal he wanted to bring home and perhaps even knew what position he would like to see the animal in for the rest of his life. But if not, the taxidermist usually has sample poses in his studio and many suggested poses in his catalog. Some hunters like just heads. Some include the whole front quarter of the animal so it looks as if it is coming straight through the wall into the room. A puma crouching in the rafters overhead or a leopard springing from the wall onto the back of a running deer makes a spine-tingling conversation piece. The taxidermist can put the animal dummy into almost any position the hunter can think of. Leaping animals are reinforced with steel bars inside. Sometimes the bars are cleverly hidden inside a piece of log or a fake rock.

A good taxidermist must be a well-informed naturalist, according to Coloman Jonas, who founded a taxidermy company in Denver, Colorado, before the days of Carl Akeley's African trophies. Mr. Jonas' company has its own large natural history reference library that includes books, all the field notes and measurements made on the spot, photographs, models, casts, and scale drawings of animals it has made up. It also has a "skeleton bank." But more important than even these essentials is what the founder had in mind originally. The taxidermist must be an artist who knows animals—the way the mule deer's ears fan out when he is listening to the hunter's "silent" approach; the contentedly curling tail of the puma when he is happily digesting a satisfying meal; the crouched-down stalking position of the wolf.

Sometimes a fisherman catches one that he knows "they'll never believe at home." So he plans to have it mounted. Or the fisherman may be a researcher who has caught a strange fish that he wants to preserve for science. At any rate, fish lose their color very fast, and almost as fast, they begin to shrink, curl up, and smell. An angler who plans to save a fish for posterity should immediately draw its outline on a large piece of paper and mark down, the color details, which will soon be gone. Then the fish is cut open on the side—not slit through the belly as if it were being filleted. The skin should then peel off, and it is salted—on the inside only. After it lies flat a day, the skin can be rolled up in a piece of paper and mailed, in a box or a can with air holes, to the taxidermist.

No such luck for the museum that wants a specimen of the blue whale—the largest mammal. So far no one has found a way to separate its skin from the blubber, and the skin cannot be mounted. A dummy is the only way to display this creature, and the Smithsonian Institution in Washington, D.C., spent more than two years on measurements and statistical studies, sketches, and designs of different whale positions before building their blue whale. Any museum that wants a blue whale had better find some space first—they come close to one hundred feet long. The Smithsonian's is made of fiber glass cloth, painted blue, stretched over a huge frame thirty feet above the floor.

A quite different kind of animal dummy is the decoy—an imitation specimen set out to lure the real creature for huntsmen or scientists.

Ducks make it tough for decoy artists. Ducks have excellent eyesight and can spot from high up a bright-colored line that anchors a decoy to the pond bottom. They are suspicious of worn-out decoys, those missing an eye, and any that do not ride on the water exactly as a duck rides. They are also suspicious of newly painted decoys early in the season when ducks themselves are in drab colors, yet if decoys do not look brighter by the time real ducks grow more colorful plumage, they are passed over quickly. No intelligent canvasback duck would join a group of canvasback decoys anchored in shallow water, because they are

46

Every kind of animal is found in the form-making plant

divers and stay in deeper water. For the same reason, no mallard or pin-tailed duck will swoop down to join a mallard decoy anchored in deep water, because they are dippers rather than divers. A duck may look down on one of his favorite spots one windy day. It is filled with "his kind" of duck—or are they? The duck would never have stopped in that spot with the wind blowing from that direction, so why did they? He swoops around, keeping well out of range, until he catches a glint of sun on a man's upturned face.

Making duck dummies is one of America's oldest folk arts. The Indians began it by stuffing a skinned duck with straw or mud. Unfortunately the stuffing did not last as long as the season for hunting ducks. White cedar or white pine, the Indians found, lasted much longer, floated more like real ducks, and could be painted to match any ducks they wanted to catch. But when the colonists arrived and the number of duck hunters multiplied faster than the ducks, finding good decoys was not easy. A good decoy

carver might turn out five hundred in his lifetime, but each duck hunter might need a dozen decoys! Besides, this was a job for specialists. Chesapeake Bay decoys needed to be solid and weighted especially to fit them for work in wind and waves, but decoys for the marshes of New Jersey worked better if they were hollow. To add to the problem, the ducks themselves became much more wary as they flew southward along the Atlantic flyway. More people settling in the warmer climates south of Canada meant just one thing to ducks—more hunters.

Since duck-hunting over decoys is not easy, some hunters might feel sorry for a group of men who recently had to pay over two thousand dollars in fines for using what they thought were the ideal decoys, real live ducks, with an anchor line tied to one leg. But the law is on the side of the hunted, and using live ducks as bait to fool more live ducks into coming closer is against the rules. If game wardens did not protect wild animals, there soon would be none left to protect.

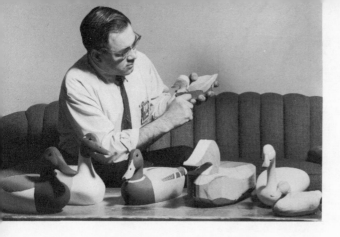

Hand carving duck decoys is a genuine American folk art. Wes Gordeuk of Connecticut uses only a penknife

WES GORDEUK
PHOTOGRAPHS BY DUFFY

Most beagle dogs have good reason to be grateful to beagle dummies, however. Real beagles were being used to test long-lasting radioisotopes in the body—a test that would eventually save many human lives. But in order for the researcher to test the isotopes in the body throughout a long period of time, it would be necessary to destroy one of the dogs each time a test was made. Then someone thought of making a phantom dog like the one that is used to test radioactive materials in the human body.

The Beagle Phantom is molded in the rubber around a real beagle skeleton. Then he is sectioned off like a loaf of bread. Any single section can be lifted out for study. A capsule of plutonium or some other radioactive substance can be inserted directly into one of the holes in each slice. The Beagle Phantom can also be used for studies involving external radiation and other tests that used to involve the destruction of a live dog. The Beagle Phantom may be man's best friend's best friend.

The Beagle Phantom is a friend in deed

ALDERSON RESEARCH LABORATORIES, INC.

48

5

Medical Teachers' Pets

PATIENT PATIENTS

SIM LIES on the operating table. His left arm is stretched out and fluid drips into his veins to keep him from getting dehydrated. A stethoscope is taped over his heart so the doctor can listen to the heartbeat at any time. A blood pressure cuff attached to his right arm is being monitored by a medical student.

The doctor has just given Sim a muscle relaxant and now Sim's breathing is being done for him by machine. The anesthetic begins to flow through the tube inserted in his trachea.

"Blood pressure is 70 over 40," warns the medical student.

Sim's muscles begin twitching. His eyes fly open and a frown creases his forehead. He tries to fight the tube in his throat.

"He's gagging," a worried nurse reports.

Suddenly Sim is still. The doctor listens through the stethoscope for the heartbeat that is no longer there.

"He's dead," says the doctor. "What did I do wrong?"

Fortunately Sim is only a manikin.

The doctor learns from his instructor what his patient died from. In this case, the doctor had not checked his patient's chart carefully enough to see that Sim was allergic to certain kinds of anesthetics and had died from the reaction. It is a mistake the doctor will never make again. But a few minutes

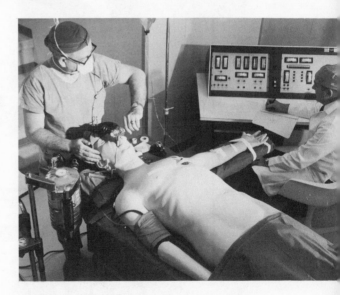

Sim I allows two of his makers to try him out. Dr. J. S. Denson prepares to operate while Paul Clark checks Sim's brain, the computer

AEROJET-GENERAL CORP.

later, Sim is "alive" again and ready to undergo his next operation with another beginning doctor.

Doctors have not always had such cooperative patients as Sim to practice on. For centuries there were only two kinds of patients—live ones and dead ones. From the dead ones doctors could learn anatomy and not much more. With the live ones, they could practice only the skills they already knew well. It was not ethical to experiment with very sick people or try new ideas on live patients. And there was never a chance for young doctors or medical students to see "interesting cases" or take part in a real emergency that had "interesting complications." How was a new doctor to learn if not from his experiences?

For that matter, how could nurses learn their jobs? Sometimes they were allowed to nurse charity or mental patients, but a nurse had to perfect many skills before she was moved on to nurse the "paying" patients. In some hospitals nurses spent years doing the dirty work of the hospital before they had enough experience to call themselves nurses. No one wanted to volunteer to be a learner's first patient—not even for free. The only other way nurses

An electronic eye view of Sim's operation

AEROJET-GENERAL CORP.

could learn their jobs was to practice on each other—a method that was understandably unpopular with the nurses. Yet their patients expected them to know exactly what to do and how to do it. They had to learn somehow.

A little girl is brought into the emergency room in a deep sleep. From her hysterical mother, nurses learn the child was found lying on the bedroom floor. There was an empty bottle of sleeping pills beside her.

"I hardly ever used them. I just kept them in a bedside table in case I ever needed them," the mother sobs.

The nurses try to calm the mother, but they have no time to waste. Every second the poison stays in the child's stomach lessens her chance to live.

Suppose now that the nurses look helplessly at each other. They have read all about how to pump out a child's stomach, but none of them want to help because they have never really done it! They may know exactly what supplies are needed to save the child's life, but unless the stomach pump is used immediately, it will not do this child any good at all.

This sort of thing does not happen in hospitals, because medical persons are trained before they ever see such an emergency. Each nurse and doctor knows exactly how to carry out the job without panic because they have all done it many times before. On a dummy.

Nurses—and patients too—have Mrs. Chase to thank for that. The

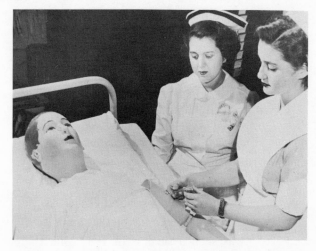

Mrs. Chase never complains—not even about shots

mother of five children, the real Mrs. Chase and her doctor-husband lived in Pawtucket, Rhode Island, in 1880. One day, while comforting a child whose favorite doll had just lost its delicate bisque china head, Mrs. Chase lost patience with such easily broken toys.

"Dolls are to be played with and loved," she thought aloud. "There is no reason why they have to be so fragile."

Mrs. Chase made a doll with a tough painted head and unbreakable arms and legs. The doll was such a success that Mrs. Chase was soon voted champion dollmaker by all her friends' children.

"Why couldn't you make a large adult-sized doll just the same way?" suggested a friend who was the instructor of nurses in a nearby Connecticut hospital. Mrs. Chase and her husband

51

began making patterns. The doll should be lightweight, because it had to be moved around a lot. Also it would be used to practice bandaging, so the "skin" should not be too slippery. It should have various inside passages and outlets like the human body, so nurses could practice the complicated techniques used with very sick persons.

The Chase hospital doll, called Mrs. Chase at most hospitals she lives in, was such a success in 1911 that there had to be a Mr. Chase and a Baby Chase too. None of the family claim to be beauties. They do not go in for dynel hair and glass eyes as so many dummies do. Their success is due to their long lives and rugged constitutions. The fact that many a hospital is still using its original Mrs. Chase doll to train its nurses is proof enough that the Chases come from hardy New England stock.

Today Mrs. Chase's torso is strongly built and covered with a vinyl plastic skin that can't be spoiled by the water or medicines that may spill all over it. The arms, fingers, legs, and toes are flexible vinyl so that they are easy to bandage. Mrs. Chase even has two places where a nurse can practice giving shots.

Mr. and Mrs. Chase's blank expressions have overlooked all the mistakes made by the nurses, nurses' aides, and practical nurses that they have helped to train. Always being The First Patient for every nervous trainee has its hazards—and the Chases don't always come through smiling. But repairs are easily made and they are back on the job quickly.

Even such a simple-sounding job as making the bed is not so simple if the patient in it cannot move. Nurses learn to make the bed around Mrs. Chase without moving her more than once. Positioning Mrs. Chase in a chair or bed so she will not drop over and have a bad fall can be as important as more dramatic jobs in nursing. Later, when the nurse cares for a patient with brain damage, she learns that not all humans can be expected to sit upright in a chair. Some slide down and fall over just as the listless Mrs. Chase did during their practice days. Learning to pack pillows around Mrs. Chase may save a real patient's life someday.

Baby Chase has been a baby for sixty years, teaching nurses, pediatricians, and fumble-fingered fathers. Most hospitals have "school" for new mothers and fathers either before or just after the new baby's arrival. The new parents learn to bathe their baby, take his temperature, feed him, and change diapers. Many parents have never touched a new baby before they have their own. Baby Chase's vinyl-coated nylon cloth body resists spilled milk formula and survives diaper-pin jabs. His nose and ear passages are just like the real baby's, so that parents can learn how to clean them out with cotton swabs dipped in baby oil. His legs and arms move freely like the real baby's, so that when the new parents get home they can handle their own baby without frightening the infant. Babies react immediately when they are picked up clumsily.

But Baby Chase's main job is not teaching new parents. He trains nurses to care for infants and young children —both sick and well. For this reason, Baby Chase comes in four sizes—newborn, three months, one year, and four years. Even though a nurse may be skilled taking care of adults, she enters an entirely new world when she takes care of children and infants.

Another patient patient in the infant nursery is Anne Baby. She is designed especially to teach parents and nurses to care for a well infant. A healthy two weeks old, Anne weighs in at 6½ pounds and is 21 inches long. At the school for new parents, fathers used to practice with toy dolls. But when they took their new baby home and held him, they discovered that real babies are not at all like a doll. For one thing, a baby's head is the heaviest part. But a doll's head is usually very lightweight. Anne Baby's head is not only heavy, but like a real baby her neck must be supported when she is lifted or held. Anne has the soft spot at the top of her head that closes over in a real baby as he grows older. Her arms and legs flop like a baby's, too, instead of sticking out at awkward angles like a doll's. When Anne is raised slightly by her heels to change her diaper, her knees stretch naturally. She can also soil her diaper as realistically as the human model!

Anne Baby travels in a baby bathtub and wears real clothes. She teaches baby care to nurses and new parents, but she has found that school children need to learn about baby care too. She teaches in elementary schools where many children have baby sisters and brothers to take care of while their parents are at work. She also teaches in secondary schools where many of the students will be earning their own money by baby-sitting. Baby manikins are needed everywhere in the world to teach mothers in undeveloped countries how to keep their children alive and well. In many lands, half the babies die before they are even one year old.

Dexter is a dental volunteer, a job

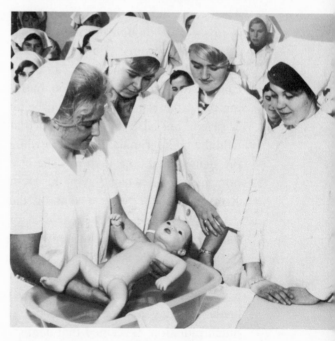

A class learns about infant care from Anne Baby

LAERDAL MEDICAL CORP.

53

no one else wants. One of the courses a dentist must study is radiography, or how to take photographs with the X-ray machine. Before X-ray was discovered, the dentist had to rely on his patient to point out "which tooth hurt." Then he yanked it out. Unfortunately for the patient—and maybe the dentist too—the tooth pulled out was not always the one that caused the trouble. Sometimes teeth ache with a sympathetic pain or a tooth with a dying nerve may seem to hurt in several places before an ache settles down in one place. Dentists, as well as patients, were very glad when X-ray came along to show at a glance just which tooth was causing the trouble.

At first dentists learned to use the machine by X-raying each other's teeth. Then came the startling discovery that X-rays—even though invisible—could be very dangerous. Too much radiation building up in the body can cause cancer. Not only was radiation building up in the jaws of the person being X-rayed, but also in the finger that held the photographic film steady while the dentist took the picture. There is no danger for a person having his teeth X-rayed once or twice a year by the dentist, but there was a great deal of danger when a class full of dentists all X-rayed each other's jaws several times. Radiation does not disappear in a person's body. It builds up until suddenly one day a person has had too much radiation. It seemed that dentists might have to learn about radiography from a book and never have a chance

to try it on real patients until they had graduated from dental school. Even then, it was not something they could learn overnight. It takes practice to make clear X-ray photographs. Just in time Dexter came along.

Dexter's real name is Dental X-ray Teaching and Training Replica #2, or Dxttr-II. But the shorter name suits him best, perhaps because Dexter is so short himself. He is really only a head and neck, with an extension gadget like a finger to hold the X-ray film firmly in place in his mouth. But Dexter has one feature that all dentists wish their patients had—a lever on top of his head to make him open his mouth when told to. There is also a device to keep him from snapping his mouth shut suddenly and biting.

Dexter fastens onto the back of a dental chair. But just because he is all head is no reason to think he has nothing else. His skull is a real human skull imported from Asia. There the diet of many vegetables and little meat has left the skull's original owner with unusually good teeth. A skull is a reject if more than two molars are missing or the teeth are in bad shape. After all, Dexter's whole reason for existing is to give dentists a chance to practice taking X-rays of teeth! The teeth are coated with plastic to keep them from loosening and falling out. Something like "rubber bumpers" are built up on the back molars to protect Dexter's valuable teeth—just in case the dentist accidentally disengages the ratchet device that keeps Dexter from biting. If

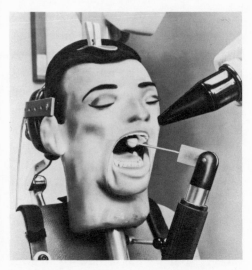

Dexter, the patient every dentist would like

ALDERSON RESEARCH LABORATORIES, INC.

his mouth snapped shut suddenly, his teeth might get broken, and the dentist might have a time explaining how he was bitten by a dummy.

Dexter's skull is filled with a plastic material except for the mouth area. Hollows in the cheeks and eyes are filled in with rubber and plastic foam. Then the skull is covered with a latex skin and the hair is painted on. His lips, cheeks, and tongue are plastic, but they are as pliable as a human's. His chin is specially made so his mouth can open realistically. Because metal parts would show up on X-rays and look confusing in the background, all movable parts that would be in the way are made of plastic.

Dexter is one dummy that is really an individual. Since each skull came from a different person instead of all coming out of the same mold, each

Dexter looks slightly different. The skin is fitted to each particular skull. Then Dexter is given his "social security number." The manufacturer issues a number for each Dxttr-II and stores under that number the molds that were used to make his face. If he is ever damaged, he can be immediately refitted with perfectly matching parts.

If doctors ever get together to vote for their favorite patient, Sim will certainly come at the top of the list. Real patients are hardly more "human" than Sim.

Every person who ever had his tonsils out is thankful that someone discovered anesthesia. There was no rush for it after one medical man suggested using it in 1800. Actually not until forty-four years later did a dentist, Horace Wells, have to pull his own tooth. The prospect so frightened him that he was about to try anything that might help. The anesthetic he chose was nitrous oxide—better known as laughing gas—and after he had pulled out his tooth he was really happy. In no time at all, everyone heard about the success of this anesthetic. People who had been putting off trips to the dentist for years suddenly showed up to make appointments.

But there were still some problems before anesthetics could be used for everything and everyone. Doctors had to learn how much anesthetic was needed to be effective and at what point it became dangerous. The amount was different for each person. A patient might survive an operation only to be in worse condition when the anesthetic made him sick. Medical men were not satisfied until they had found a safer way to give anesthesia.

The newest way of giving anesthesia is by passing a tube into the trachea. The gas then flows through the tube. But that sounds deceivingly simple. It is not easy. Inserting the tube into the trachea can be dangerous until the anesthesiologist learns to do it well. And that is where the problem lies. How can he learn to do it well when it takes about eighteen tries? No volunteers are eager to be among the first seventeen people the anesthesiologist practices on.

There were dummies with "throats" for anesthesiologists to practice on, but just learning to push the tube down the trachea was not the only problem. Doctors must also watch many of the life signs of their patient and check the proper amount of anesthetic for each person at the same time. Many emergencies may happen in the operating room, and anesthesiologists, who are also doctors, must be ready to make the right decisions the first time. Instructors wondered how their doctor students would ever learn to make all the right decisions. So when a computer expert happened to ask what computers could do for medicine, the idea for Sim I was born.

Sim the First seems so human that medical people have a hard time remembering he is not. He breathes and has a heartbeat. A pulse beats in his carotid artery (neck) and temporal artery (head). His eyes open and close and the pupils can change in size. A hinged jaw opens to show his tongue, teeth, and bronchial tubes. His skin is urethane and vinyl, but it looks and feels like the real thing. Inside, however, Sim's anatomy is nothing like a person's.

He is filled with mechanisms to make his lungs, chest, and abdomen move naturally as he breathes. His arteries pulsate and his face can change expression. Sim II is much like his brother, but he has a new right arm. "Blood samples" can be drawn from his veins and a doctor can "feel" the pulse, muscle, nerves, and bone in the new arm. A nurse just learning to give injections in Sim II's right arm may hit a nerve. If she does, Sim II will jerk, and probably frown too.

But what really sets Sim apart from other dummies is his brain. He is connected to a computer and programmed to make the same responses a human patient might make. In fact he surprised his creators once by doing something he had not even been programmed to do. When certain buttons were pushed at the computer console, Sim began a special type of breathing. The doctors looked up in amazement.

"Why was he breathing like that? Was he programmed to do that too?" one doctor asked. The answer was simple, but complex too. Sim's breathing had followed a natural chain of events that occurred after the first buttons were pushed. A human patient having all the first symptoms would

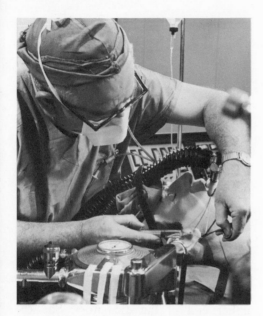

The tube carries the anesthetic directly into Sim's trachea

have followed the same pattern with that same type of on-again, off-again breathing. So Sim did too.

Sim's main job is to put the doctor student through dozens of drastic emergencies. The instructor, sitting at the computer console, has all Sim's reactions and symptoms at his fingertips. While the poor student tries to remember all his medical school learning at the same time, the instructor has a good chance to see how clearly this doctor-to-be can think in a crisis.

Joe, a fourth-year student, is told to perform an endotracheal intubation. He knows that means to put the tube down the patient's trachea. He also knows exactly how to do it. He has read how dozens of times and he has already put the tube down Sim's throat twice before. The last time it slid down beautifully. Joe is confident this morning. But the teacher is not about to let Joe get smug this early in his career. Emergencies do happen, and it is time for Joe to see how he faces a real one.

Deftly, Joe inserts the tube. Sim's blood pressure is good, although it has changed from what it was a few minutes ago. Joe smiles as he checks the strong, rhythmic heartbeat. Then suddenly Sim begins to jerk. He is trying to cough, but without enough air in his lungs the action is more like a bucking bronco. Joe increases the oxygen. Sim is only beginning to be difficult.

Before the session is over, Sim has a dangerous reaction to one of the drugs. He has severe muscle twitchings. His jaw tenses so tightly that he almost bites the anesthesia tube in half. His breathing changes from shallow to rapid to no breathing at all. The blood pressure shoots downward rapidly. Finally Sim's heart beats in a dozen different irregular patterns and then stops completely. Sim wins again!

But Sim has pulled only a few of his many tricks on Joe. His supply of surprises is as full of possibilities as a human's. As for Joe—he is exhausted. But at least he did not lose his head and he thinks next time he'll be more prepared when Sim starts playing tricks. Sim won't win the game next time. The instructor at the console presses a button, and Sim, lying arm outstretched on the table, smiles.

6

It's a Dummy World
THE TIRELESS ONES

POLITENESS is so important in Japan that even the dummies have good manners. Visitors to Tokyo's Mitsukoshi Department Store had always been greeted by a smiling girl who stood near the escalator. Bowing and offering her hand, she said, "Thank you for coming" and "Watch your step" as she helped customers on and off the moving stairs. The job was tiresome and the prestige was small. All a girl needed to qualify for the job was good manners. Someone mentioned even a dummy could do the job.

Recently, when employers could not find the type of girl they wanted, that is just what happened. The store's executive staff felt their customers could now cope with getting on and off the escalators without the helping hand. But for them not to hear the traditional words of welcome to the store—that was a custom too deeply rooted to be dropped so casually.

"Our customers would be insecure," some executives worried. "Our number one motto is Service!"

So today, until she is replaced by a human, a pleasant-faced dummy, dressed in the miniskirted uniform that is worn by all the salesgirls, stands at either end of the escalators. She repeats over and over, "Irashaimase. . . . Watch your step. . . ." Most customers do not even know this cute doll is a dummy.

If dummies ever traced their ancestry, a good many of them would go back as far as scarecrows. Every country has had its trouble with birds that wanted the same food man wanted. And every country has found that scarecrows have a natural talent for solving that problem. But even scarecrows may lose their jobs if they are not careful. In some fields they are being replaced by evil-smelling chemical repellants or clackety noisemakers that are either run mechanically or moved by the wind.

Senji Kataoka works for the Japanese Ministry of Agriculture. Recently he was so concerned over the disappearance of scarecrows in his country that he became president—and only member—of the Japan Scarecrow Institute. Kataoka says the farmers should make more beautiful and creative scarecrows to frighten away the sparrows that help themselves to the rice crop. He became interested in scarecrows because he once had to make an official survey to see how good a job was done by the dummies. He learned not only that scarecrows performed their jobs better than any mechanical or chemical means but also that they added much to their country's culture. Just after World War II, many Japanese scarecrows wore old uniforms. But today they show the prosperity that has come to their land, for they appear wearing business suits and flapping kimonos.

Another kind of silent sentinel has joined the scarecrow. There is a bridge on the highway to Kyoto where too many motorists have had accidents. Police recognized the danger where the road suddenly curves around onto the bridge, but so far no warning sign had ever scared speeding motorists enough to slow them down in time. Now the approaching driver is shaken when he sees a traffic policeman ahead waiting just for him. Immediately, he hits the brakes. By the time he learns that he has been fooled by a dummy policeman, it is too late to speed up again. At night drivers see only the luminous eyes and belt, but it's enough to make the brakes squeal just before the curve.

It was a dark night when Silent Sam was born. Suddenly a car's headlights glowed on something that should not have been on the road. The driver

Silent Sam's flag is ten feet from the ground and can be seen 4,000 feet away
QUEENS DEVICES, INC.

slammed on his brakes. The car rocked a bit and slid to a stop just a few feet away from an unmarked barricade extending into the road. A road construction gang had gone home, leaving the barriers at the road's edge without lights or even flags to warn oncoming cars. Fortunately, the driver of the car was not only a creative man, but one who cared for his fellow humans. Martin Kaltman began planning a robot that would work nonunion hours for no wages, that would not complain about the weather or the lack of coffee breaks.

The result is Silent Sam. For the price of an occasional battery recharge, Sam will wave his red flag at motorists all day or all night. Dressed in a construction worker's red steel helmet and

59

blue coveralls, he stands six feet tall, but his flag hand is much higher. Thanks to Sam, a valuable workman is released from a dull type of job to help with the road repairs instead.

Sam's job is not all dull routine. When one driver on the Pennsylvania Turnpike suddenly saw Sam waving a red flag at him, with a swift pass of his automobile, he took off Sam's waving arm at the shoulder. Sam had cost almost a thousand dollars, and now that he had been laid off the job to recover from his experience and to get a new arm, a real man must be paid to take his place. That same careless driver probably wonders why turnpike fees go up in price.

During one winter when it was too cold in the north to work on repairing roads, a pair of Silent Sams from Philadelphia started a new occupation. About mid-November, the two Sams disappeared for a while. Rumor was that they were "seeing their tailors." When they next appeared, their shiny red workman's helmets were matched with bright red Santa Claus suits. Perched on top of the toll booths of two Delaware River bridges, the two Sams waved holiday greetings to startled motorists. Their right arms were still waving up and down, but instead of carrying flags, their hands held silver bells.

Another role for dummies developed because people expect much more of clothes than they used to—perhaps because man has moved into strange new environments that can often be harsh

in temperatures. Looking right is not nearly so important as being comfortable and safe. Men in the Arctic must wear mittens instead of gloves because it is almost impossible to keep separated fingers warm enough, even in the most scientifically designed gloves. Scouts on camping trips need sleeping bags that will keep them from freezing in case the temperature plunges to an unexpected low during

Underwear for a new environment—a doctor describes the long johns worn by Frank Borman and James A. Lovell, Jr., aboard Gemini VII

NASA

60

the night. Skiers need parkas, gloves, and boots that will protect them from frostbite in case they are injured and have to lie in the snow waiting for rescue. Hikers insist on clothing that can be rainproof, yet lightweight enough to carry on their backs. Servicemen need special types of clothing to give them the most protection with the least amount of discomfort and weight. Scuba divers need suits to protect them from exposure to chilly water. Thousands of clothing needs are met every day. But very few people know they owe many of their modern clothing comforts to a dummy.

It is early afternoon and a cargo plane is making a routine flight out of Vietnam. Suddenly a burst of enemy fire strikes the gas tanks. The pilot steers out over water. Chances of rescue are better there than in enemy-filled territory. He signals his crew to bail out while he grapples with a lurching airplane. At the last moment, he too bails out. His chute opens and jerks him to a sudden stop in the sky. He watches his burning plane crash into the sea far below.

The water temperature down there must be about 75°F. But there is wind and waves, which will make it seem colder. The pilot remembers summer days of swimming in the Atlantic Ocean when the temperature was 75°F. and it didn't seem cold. But he has been briefed on the seriousness of being in water of that temperature for long periods. It will be getting dark in five hours. If rescue does not arrive

The copper man gets plugged in for another day's work

within eight to twelve hours, many of his crewmen who are floating now in the water below him are not going to make it.

The pilot glances down at the new type of wet suit he and the crew were ordered to put on just before takeoff an hour earlier. The men griped a lot because the suit was harder to move around in and uncomfortably hot in the humid Vietnamese weather. But they had no choice and they are all wearing the new suits. One glance at a world map had shown that there was a 67 percent chance that a plane might

61

have to be ditched in water 77°F. or colder. As the pilot drops into the water and releases his chute, his crewmen all cheer. At least they are all together. And—so far—they are all still alive.

At this moment, none of the men would be at all relieved to know that their lives now depend on the advice of a dummy—the copper man.

The copper man is the size of a U.S. Army infantryman. He is hollow inside, but his "skin" is wired for heat. At nineteen different places on his body, thermocouples measure his skin temperature. When the copper man is dressed in specially designed clothing and subjected to specified conditions, the medical researchers can tell by his temperature how that clothing is going to affect a human under the same conditions. But there are two important types of clothing for him to test—the type that is designed for cold climates, when the wearer usually does not sweat, and the type designed for hot weather, when the sweating factor makes a great deal of difference.

When hot weather clothing is tested, the copper man wears his "sweating skin." This is a cotton skin that covers the manikin. When the cotton skin is wetted, researchers can tell how much the uniform he wears will interfere with his evaporative cooling-off process— his sweating. This measures the impermeability, and therefore the comfort on a hot day, of the clothing.

When a man is resting, he produces about 70 kilocalories (kcal) of heat an

The copper man wears his "sweating skin" to test a new raincoat

hour. This is a base for measuring the heat his body produces. If the same man were to exercise, he would produce anywhere from 350 to 700 kcal an hour. No man could stand such heat for a long time if it were not for sweating. Sweating cools the body by producing droplets of water on the skin. As the drops of water evaporate in the air, the skin is cooled. But if the clothing is impermeable, the air will not go through it. There is no evaporation and the skin grows hotter than ever. What is worse, the body goes on sweating and loses a great deal of water. Before very long, the person will drop from heat exhaustion—all because of the clothing he wears.

When three different types of suits were designed to protect the man who has to float in cold water waiting to be rescued, medical researchers from the Army, Navy, and Air Force all wanted to know which kind was the best. No one was willing to risk even one pilot's life to find out. This was a job for the copper man. With his "sweating skin" on, he could tell just how a human would feel in each of the three suits.

One was a dry suit and much more comfortable to wear in the air than either of the other two. But while the dry suit felt good in the air and the pilot could have worn it more comfortably for his ordinary flying duties, it was not being tested for wearing comfort alone. The main purpose of the new suit was to protect the flyers in case of an emergency dunking. And that particular suit compressed as soon as it was in water until the insulation was hardly effective at all. Also, if the wearer had torn the suit getting out of his plane, which was quite possible, the material would have given him even less protection.

Soon the copper man showed the researchers which of the remaining two —both wet suits—was the best. His reactions favored the same wet suit

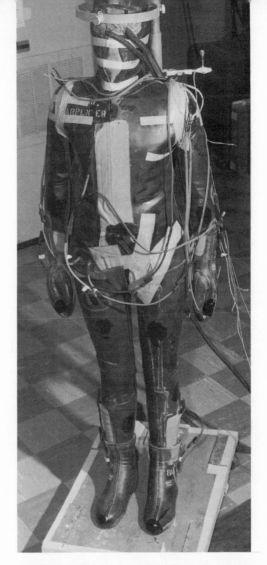

Scott Carpenter's wet suit, worn on Sea Lab II, is tested by the copper man

worn by the crew of the cargo plane when they were forced to ditch in the 75°F. water off Vietnam. When the airmen were rescued, there were headlines in several local hometown newspapers. The articles mentioned the protective clothing that had kept them comfortable during the hours they waited for rescue. But no paper mentioned the copper man.

During the Trojan War, 3100 years ago, soldiers complained loudly about the heavy loads they had to carry. Their armor weighed eighty pounds, and no one had yet thought of putting men on horses to lighten their burdens. Except for the armor worn by knights in the Middle Ages, who did ride horseback, no other soldiers in history have had to carry so much weight. When extremely heavy loads are carried by soldiers, they burn about ten times the energy they ordinarily do. This slows them down considerably and can have much to do with winning or losing a battle.

Today's soldier is helped by the copper man, who measures a load by telling medical researchers how much energy he burns up trying to carry it. The temperature of the room can be regulated to that of the environment the soldier will be marching in, perhaps 85°F. with the humidity at 75 percent. Then the researchers will know how long a soldier can stand up under the load they plan. It's better for the copper man to sweat and groan under the load than for a rifle platoon of soldiers to collapse at the very moment when their lives may depend on their being alert.

The copper man does not make the headlines. Testing special items of clothing is just his ordinary everyday job. There is always something new to try out. One is a material with tiny wires woven in it to supply heat. It can be used in making gloves. Another suit carries its own battery to provide heat for several hours. Some of the radioisotopes may someday be used to provide heat. They weigh only a few grams, but they are radioactive. The shielding that would be necessary to protect the wearer would add greatly to the weight of such a suit. The space program also provides many ideas such as a water-conditioned suit made of tiny plastic water pipes. On a hot day, cool water could circulate through the same pipes that provide warm heating for a cold day.

At the rate new ideas are showing up, the copper man will not be out of a job for a long time.

7

Dummy Bits and Pieces

THE INSIDE STORY

No PERSON TODAY would think of studying pictures of the body's various organs and then performing an operation on a living human. But that is exactly what was expected of a surgeon in the sixteenth century.

Surgeons ranked several notches below a doctor in those days—and no wonder! Their successful operations were none too plentiful and any patient surviving a serious one was more likely to give the credit to a miracle rather than to any skill the surgeon had. A dummy torso was the missing tool, but no one could have made one for the simple reason that no one knew what the human body looked like inside. And that includes the doctors.

"Who needs to look at a body?" asked the old doctors. "We have the works of Galen."

Galen, a Greek physician to several Roman emperors, had written books in the second century A.D. that contained all the information about the body that it seemed any doctor should ever need. He had described his dissections clearly and accurately. Over thirteen hundred years later, his books were still the authority on anatomy.

Religion and medicine were not friends—and religion kept doctors from dissecting human bodies. Mohammedan surgeons were forbidden by the Koran; Christians by papal edicts; and Orientals by a belief in ancestor worship. The human body carried all its secrets with it to the grave. The best medical schools were in Italy, and even there only one dead body could be dissected each year. The audience was limited to twenty persons and they were chosen on the basis of where they came from—five from Lombardy, four from Rome, three from Bologna, four from Tuscany, and so on. Other countries were worse. By the fifteenth century, Italy was about the only country where a doctor could see what the human body looked like.

But a rebel, Vesalius, was born in Belgium in 1514. The boy dissected every dead mouse, cat, and dog he could get his hands on, fully expecting that he would learn about humans as soon as he reached medical school. But no, it was more cats and dogs at school in Belgium. One day Vesalius and some friends looked longingly on the body of a criminal hanging outside the city walls, and that night, they cut him down. But before the criminal could make his contribution to science, the boys were arrested. Vesalius wisely left the country for medical school in Paris. There it was more cats and dogs —and anatomy from Galen's books. By now Vesalius learned that doctors were not the only ones who wanted to know what made the human body tick—so did artists. In Italy, artists such as Michelangelo and Leonardo da Vinci had performed many dissections on their own. Vesalius promptly enrolled in medical school at Padua near Venice. He became a doctor on December 5, 1537, and the next day was made professor of surgery there. At last, Vesalius had all the bodies he needed.

While Vesalius dissected to his heart's content, his best friend, Stephan Van Calcar, illustrated each part removed. Only then did Vesalius find out why he really had not trusted the anatomy of Galen all along. Galen had not been dissecting humans at all. His book illustrated only the anatomy of pigs and monkeys!

"He's a crazy fool poisoning the air of Europe with his vaporings," said his old teacher of dog and cat anatomy in Paris when Vesalius published the first book on human anatomy. But other doctors agreed that the way anatomy was being taught to doctors and sur-

A dummy cannot always pull himself together—he needs help

TIMES-CHRONICLE, JENKINTOWN, PA.

geons really left something to be desired —especially by the patient! Several centuries would pass, however, before any medical men knew enough about the human body to create a dummy torso.

The best way to teach anatomy is with a dummy torso. The Talking Torso explains how to take itself apart and then proves it by really coming apart in thirty-five pieces. This human jigsaw puzzle has 650 colored and easily identifiable parts. It describes the different systems in its body, speaking through a phonograph record. Schools that buy it have a choice of getting one with Negro or white skin tone; a male,

66

a female, a sexless model, or one that has interchangeable male and female features. So that girls can learn the process by which they become mothers, the torso even comes complete with a baby. The tough, unbreakable plastic skin is guaranteed, which is more than can be said of human skin.

Children forget most easily what they hear, next what they see, but remember best what they actually experience. That's where dummy parts come in. A heart or a stomach is much easier to recognize, even in pictures, after a child has once held them in his hands. There is hardly any biological function that cannot be bought in specially built models. Children with speech defects can handle a working model four times the size of their own larynx. Because the model's vocal cords are a pliable plastic, the teacher can show children how the vocal cords

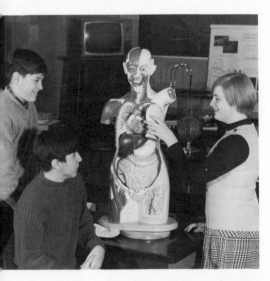

The Talking Torso instructs a biology class
DENOYER-GEPPERT, CHICAGO

open and close to change the sounds.

Some parts of the body are too small and intricate to study in life size. But dummy parts can be magnified thousands of times. A giant eye that comes apart or an eyeball with a removable lens would have been welcomed by ancient doctors. One of the most common operations was to restore vision to patients blinded by cataracts. The Assyrian doctors pressed the cataract downward with a needle so it no longer covered the cornea of the eye. But the operation was fraught with danger—and not all for the patient. The king Hammurabi had established rules for everything that might happen in his kingdom, and rules for eye operations were not neglected. A doctor should receive ten shekels for healing a man's eye, but could ask only five for healing a nobleman. He received a paltry two shekels for healing a slave. However, if the doctor's instrument slipped and the man was blinded by accident, the doctor's hands were cut off.

A model of a jawbone, showing how the teeth develop, would have come in handy in Egypt. Several mummies show that abscessed teeth were a common complaint and the cure was to drill holes through the jawbone to drain out the pus. A dummy ear that has forty parts, including a removable eardrum, would have helped ancient doctors in the days when little could be done for severe earaches. Cutting off a person's ear was one of the most common punishments for crimes like

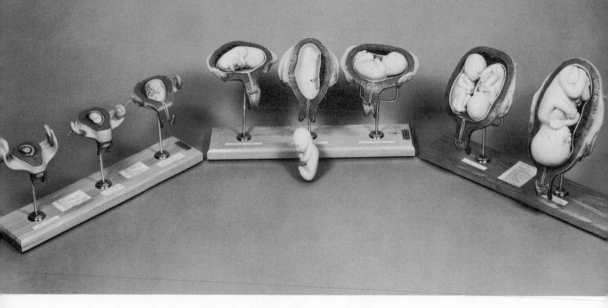

The youngest dummy of all demonstrates the progress of human development

stealing a loaf of bread. Naturally, the thinking robber thought twice about committing a crime that would leave him marked for life. Surgeons soon found there was good money in learning to sew ears back on again and many mummies show that those early transplants were successful.

Today's experiences with heart transplants put the dummy heart at the top of the list of dummy pieces needed by schools. The heart was the most misunderstood portion of anatomy all through history. Egyptians discovered the pulse almost four thousand years ago, knew its pulsations came from the heart, and knew the patient's health was measured by it. Yet for many centuries the heart was considered the seat of intelligence, because it "spoke" in so many different parts of the body. This news made it difficult for the brain, which was constantly being oper-

ated on to relieve headaches, because the head was a relatively unimportant part of the body.

But the greatest mystery the body kept hidden was the secret of blood circulation. Galen had explained it simply—the body just kept on making new blood all the time and an occasional bleeding would let out the old stuff. An Arabian doctor discovered that blood flowed through the lungs on its way from the right side of the heart to the left, but his joy at discovering such an important secret was dulled by the prospects of a shortened life. As a Mohammedan, he was forbidden by the Koran to dissect a human body, and there was no way to tell the world his discovery without revealing how he had learned about it. So the great discovery went undiscovered for the next eight hundred years.

When William Harvey's research in

68

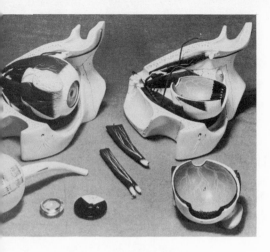

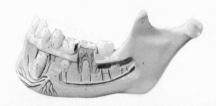

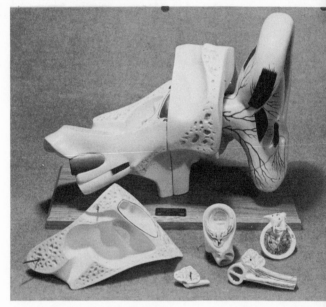

The dummy eye comes apart

This dummy heart is twice natural size

The jawbone has removable teeth

The dummy ear opens up
DENOYER-GEPPERT, CHICAGO

1615 proved that blood circulated with the heart pumping it, he was not much better off than the Arabian. Business was good—he was a professor and physician to the king—and it took him ten years to get the nerve to announce his discovery. Naturally, he was called crackbrained and thirty years passed before the idea was accepted, but at last the human body was beginning to give up some of its secrets.

A handsome pair in a Dallas, Texas, health and science museum tell the world these secrets now. Visi-Belle and Visi-Bill are specially constructed of tough see-through plastic. As they speak, the portions of the body they mention are lighted up and the organs become visible to the audience. Both dummies are anatomically correct— just like humans with transparent skin. Visi-Belle's talk has two scripts—one designed to hold the interest of children under eight years old. Inside the bodies of these two transparent dummies are exposed all the mysteries that scientists have struggled over four thousand years to explain.

8

The Victims and the Volunteers

DUMMIES IN DANGER

THE BIG DC-7 PLANE zoomed along the runway, gathering speed and straining to lift. It had traveled almost a mile and was moving about 165 mph when suddenly the action began.

First the landing gear struck on a piece of railroad rail and was knocked off completely. For a portion of a second, the plane lifted from the ground.

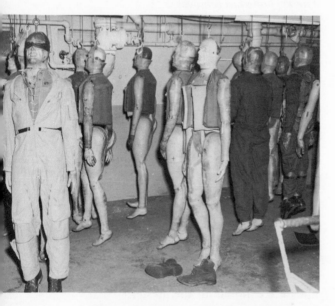

The waiting line . . . Navy volunteers waiting for the next test

At that instant, all four propellers broke off as they tore into two piles of heavy railroad ties—one pile on each side of the aircraft. One propeller blade sliced into the plane and ripped apart an unoccupied seat in the forward cabin. Then the left wing struck ground and the right wing hit two telephone poles. A trail of gasoline spilled out behind. Scraping along a slight slope, the plane once again left the ground a few feet. But now a steeper slope loomed directly ahead. Bouncing over the top of the low hill, the DC-7 finally came to a sliding stop downhill, lying on its side. For a second there was complete silence. The accident had littered debris along an 860-foot trail. It had lasted just 3½ seconds.

Firemen rushed to put out several small fires and a few larger ones that were fed by oil and gasoline from the plane's engines. When the desert dust and smoke cleared away and danger from explosion was past, the witnesses inched closer to the wreckage.

"That was perfect," beamed one man.

"Maybe not exactly as we'd planned," said another, "but a real success anyway."

"What are we waiting for? Let's take a look at the passengers," urged a man carrying a camera.

Was this a faked movie set? Or a hardhearted group of murderers? Neither. The witnesses were men whose jobs were to save lives. The DC-7 was filled with nonpaying "special invitation" passengers—all of them dummies —from the smallest, a 35-pound little girl, to the largest 200-pound man. The accident was all in the day's work. Some were there to test specially designed seats. Some were trying out seat belts, shoulder harnesses, and air bags. Some tested the way the seats were bolted to the floor of the aircraft. Even the seats themselves were being tested.

Every time a plane crashes, a thorough investigation is made. Planes are safer all the time and accidents much more rare. Investigators can piece together an entire crashed plane and find out exactly what went wrong. But there are certain types of airplane accidents that happen on the ground. These crashes were taking human lives that researchers felt should have been saved. For example, a hard landing might break the landing gear, forcing a plane to slide to a halt on its nose. Or one wing might hit the ground, spinning the plane around and around until it stopped. Or a plane making a forced landing might hit trees at the edge of a field, causing the highly in-

flammable gasoline to spill out and ignite. Such crashes should have many survivors in a planeload, but too often they did not. The U.S. Government and the airline industries wanted to find out why not.

The Federal Aviation Administration decided to stage an airplane crash of its own. It would include—in one crash—all those typical ground accidents. Each kind had actually happened recently. But before the FAA could arrange their full-scale crash test, they learned they were not the only ones interested. The U.S. Army, Navy, Air Force, NASA, and representatives from the aviation industry all had experiments of their own they wanted to test on this short plane flight.

A special runway was built, long enough so the plane could get up speed before reaching the area where the crash was to begin. Cameras both in-

Accelerometers and load links testify for the dummies after a rocket sled ride

71

side and outside would record everything that happened. To be sure that fire would not destroy the entire test plane, all but one fuel tank was filled with colored water. When the fuel tanks smashed, the dye showed where gasoline would have spilled. Only one special tank had gasoline, and the fire it caused could be extinguished quickly. The plane was painted with special markings that made it easier to follow in the photographs. The engine was run by remote control.

At last it was time to put the passengers in their seats. Of course only dummies volunteered for the trip. But they were a special type—called anthropomorphic dummies. The weight of each dummy is distributed just like a human's, so its center of gravity as it sat on the seats was like a person's. In each chest cavity is space for instruments and these dummies had them. There were accelerometers to record how fast they had moved to the front or side, up or down. Load links measured how much strain had been put on their lap belts or shoulder harnesses.

After the airplane crash the researchers recorded what had happened to everything inside the plane—from the passengers and their seats to the dishes in the galley. Some of the dummies had crashed through the seats in front of them. Some had been held firmly by their seat belts and some had not. The best rider of all seemed to have been the little girl. She was wearing a new type of harness restraint that still held her firmly at the end of the trip. But there was evidence that even she had not had a joy ride. Her right shoe was found outside the aircraft. When the researchers read some of the telemetry data from the dummies' instruments, they began to appreciate what tremendous forces press against a human in a crash. At one point, the dummy copilot hit 43G's and the pressure on his shoulder harness measured 1150 pounds!

Safety features for airplanes do not have nearly so long a history as airplanes have. When thirty-seven pilots were killed in 1910, people wondered whether they really ought to think a little more about safety. From the thousands who crashed and managed to survive, they began gathering some data. Some pilots complained that they had crashed because of a bee sting that temporarily blinded them. Since these were not the only crashes caused by insects and birds, someone finally invented a windshield. When several pilots complained that rough air had made them fall out of their seats, someone suggested that maybe the pilot's seat should be more than just a few boards he straddled with his legs dangling in the air beneath the plane. Someone else suggested tying him in with a rope. Eventually, someone invented the cockpit. Parachutes had already been invented, but they were used only for aerial circuses and thrill shows.

The earliest planes flying in World War I were so flimsy that one pilot flying higher could tear holes in the wings of the lower plane just by dropping a rock. But the possibilities in wartime were soon recognized and pilots began shooting at each other. A strange attitude developed, however, when it came to being shot down. A British, American, or French pilot had two choices when his plane was hit and flames roared back toward the cockpit. He could stay with the plane and slowly roast or he could jump over the side and end it all quickly. Parachutes were out. They were huge, bulky, and unreliable. Even though German pilots sometimes surprised the Allies by parachuting to safety, many pilots thought there was something unsporting about saving oneself. Actually the way the Germans did it, parachuting was almost as risky as the other two alternatives. The parachute

After the parachute ride—a dummy dressed in Gemini-type spacesuit waves an A-O.K.

had to be attached to the plane, and the force of the jumper triggered the chute's opening. Many times the chutes caught on the wings or tail or even the propeller. Most people were certain there could be no other way to open a parachute except by attaching it to the plane. They said that if a jumper managed to get free from the plane and began falling, he would certainly faint or be unconscious and never be able to open his own chute. Even if he should succeed, they insisted, his back would be broken by the jerk of the chute opening as he plummeted faster and faster toward the ground.

Dummies were carried aloft and dumped overboard by the dozens. Every week there was a new design or a better material or a larger canopy. Many times the dummy itself, arms and legs flailing around and tangling in the shrouds, caused a parachute to fail. Testing parachutes was no job for a dummy—at least not the kind of dummy around then. The war was all over by the time Leslie Irvin designed a parachute that a man could open by himself. Irvin bailed out of a plane at 1500 feet and astounded his fellow flyers by letting himself fall a full 500 feet before he pulled the ripcord that opened the chute. After his success, airfields demanded that no pilot leave the ground without a parachute on. Airplane safety had begun to arrive.

Today there are parachute-testing dummies without arms and legs. The chute tester is just a torso, weighing from 200 pounds up, depending on

73

how much ballast is put inside. He can take free falls without being harmed and the instruments inside him measure his fall. It was a dummy that showed the world a thing or two about jumping, especially at the lower altitudes where a man's body reaches its greatest speed about eight seconds after he leaves the plane. From that point on, he will not fall faster through the air. In fact, dummies later proved that jumpers falling from much higher altitudes actually *slow down* as they reach the lower altitude where the atmosphere is heavier. A jumper from almost any altitude slows down to around 120 mph before he opens his chute. This evidence was hard to swallow, so a real man was sent up to see if it could be true. An Army sergeant, Randall Bose, volunteered and made a free fall of 1500 feet. By 1925, free falling had become one of the most important discoveries in air safety and would save many lives twenty years later when jet planes arrived.

Long before the first jet plane left trails across the sky, researchers had begun work on the new problems the increased speed would bring. The doubters were gathering around again. Bailing out of a jet plane was completely impossible, they said. The pilot would not even be able to leave his seat. It was true that a wide turn pinned him to his seat by centrifugal force. They said the wind at 500 mph would break a man's arm or leg like a toothpick. It was true that a 500 mph wind could smash a concrete building. But

A dummy shoots through the canopy of a jet into the landing net. Note flying pieces of the jet's canopy

OFFICIAL U.S. NAVY PHOTO

researchers knew they had to find some way to escape. They were working on it and so were dummies.

While researchers were still wavering between ejecting pilots out the top of the plane or dropping them through the bottom, one pilot got in trouble. His plane lost its tail and spun crazily. Before anyone had decided which way to leave a jet, the pilot knew it was now or never. Luckily his plane was upside down and gravity helped him get out in a hurry. Luckily too, there was no tail to kill him before he could drop far enough. But he was too high up for safety. What the "you can't do it" people had said about fainting was wrong. The pilot was thinking as clearly as if he had been sitting on the

A new seat is tested on the horizontal rocket sled

U.S. AIR FORCE PHOTO

ground below. Remembering the free falling tests, the pilot rolled into a ball and dropped as fast as possible to the lower altitude where he could breathe and not freeze. Then he opened his parachute. Such near-tragedies spurred researchers on. Dummies began ejection seat tests in every position imaginable—always being caught safely in a huge net.

When the test results were announced, it seemed as if the research teams were as far from a solution as ever. But they had no doubts about it. Ejection straight up from the cockpit was the best way. The worst threat would be from the plane's tail. A pilot ejecting from a jet going 500 mph would have to leave his cockpit traveling at least 60 feet a second! There would be no time for the ejection seat to build up speed. He would have to be exploded out of the plane. That first split second outside the cockpit would be the one that counted most, because the airblasting the pilot re-

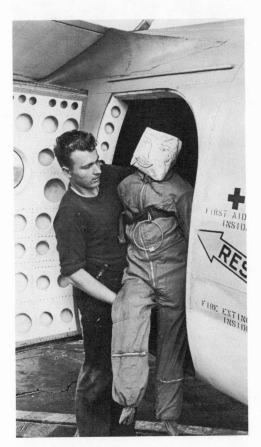

Pierre the dummy gives the Aircraft Rescue Crew a chance to polish up their quick rescue techniques

OFFICIAL U.S. NAVY PHOTO

75

ceived from the plane's speed might dash him helplessly against the tail assembly. The Germans had ejected some of their bomber pilots as early as 1939 in about the same way early circus performers were shot out of cannons. The important difference was that the circus performers had their feet next

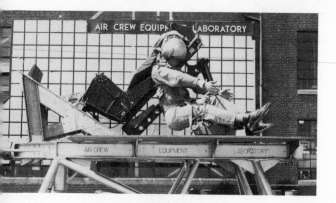

A dummy shows what happens when there is an abrupt deceleration

to the explosive. The German pilots had their spines next to the explosion point and most of the survivors had painful back injuries to show for it. Dummies could not test ejection seats for back injuries, but they could help perfect the seat itself before a human had to try it.

As soon as aeronautical engineers had computed that an ejection seat must leave the jet at 60 feet per second, the "you can't possibly do that" people were back. No man could live through it . . . the pilot's back would be broken by the explosive . . . he would be ejected at such high altitudes

that he would either freeze or die from lack of oxygen . . . he would be completely unconscious so he could not open his parachute . . . and on they went. But a man on a rocket sled proved that there is no such word as "can't" in a research field concerned with saving human lives.

The rocket sled, riding on rails cemented down in the desert sands, was catapulted by solid-propellant rockets. The tests were run with every conceivable type of seat and safety device—with dummies trying every position to find the best one. But the time came, as it always does, when the dummies had to step aside and let researchers find out whether a man could stand such a ride. The worst ride on earth was taken by Colonel John Paul Stapp, Jr., in March, 1954. He plunged 632 mph from a dead stop to a "controlled crash" stop. The crash stop took only 1.4 seconds. The forces that Stapp felt during that final second were the same that a man would feel ejecting at a 40,000 foot altitude from a plane traveling 1,000 mph! The G-force once thought to pin a pilot helplessly in his jet aircraft looked like nothing compared to the 46.2G load that Colonel Stapp felt.

Today dummies ride catapults all the time, but not that fast! The catapult is used for an endless variety of experiments. An aircraft carrier looks immense to a boy standing beside one at a dock. But to the pilot of a carrier-based plane, it looks ridiculously small in the ocean beneath him. And it is—

compared to the space he would use on a field. When he lands on the carrier, his plane is caught and brought to a quick, short stop called an abrupt deceleration. Again, when he takes off, there is too little space, so a catapult hurls his plane off to a fast start called an abrupt acceleration. At this point a plane could malfunction and drop into the ocean immediately after takeoff—another abrupt deceleration. Dummies are the testing boys for the many devices invented to save the pilots from injuries that could happen during these abrupt starts and stops. Lap belts and shoulder harnesses, form-fitting seats, inertia reels that allow the pilot freedom of motion but pull his head close to the seat back in case of a sudden jerk, protective clothing in case of fire or sudden immersion in ice-cold water, underwater seat ejection—these are only a few.

Sometimes the rocket sled is fitted with a small civilian plane fuselage—the kind of plane three or four men might use to go on a hunting trip. Tests show that anyone caught without a lap belt and harness in a small airplane is a real dummy. Often dummies try out a brand-new idea such as an air bag that inflates at the instant of a crash to hold the pilot back firmly in his seat. Many times humans ask to ride the rocket sled just for thrills. One man even offered to bring his own doctor

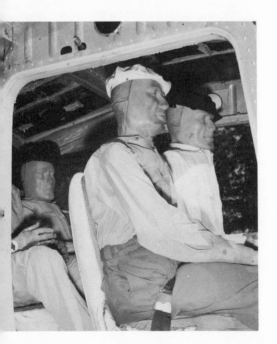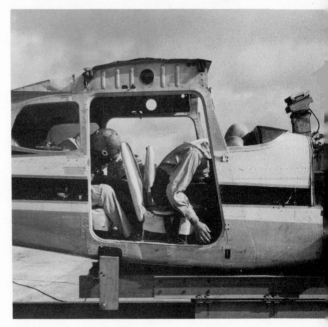

Four dummies take off on the rocket sled for a short plane ride to see whether shoulder harnesses should be recommended

FEDERAL AVIATION ADMINISTRATION
NATIONAL AVIATION FACILITIES EXPERIMENTAL CENTER

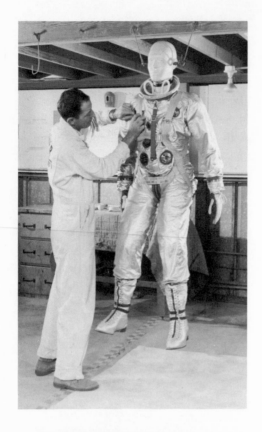

An astronaut dummy gets dressed for his big day testing the Gemini ejection seat

Strapped securely in the ejection seat, both dummy and seat receive final check

A crane lifts dummy and seat into the capsule. The ejection system will operate in the real capsule only if there is a major malfunction during lift-off or reentry

All systems are GO as the Gemini capsule waits on the rocket sled along. Luckily for the man, he was outvoted by the dummy who took the ride and was thrown off the sled accidentally. Humans used for tests are chosen carefully and receive complete medical tests first. Even then, there is always an ambulance standing by with its engine running.

Another rocket sled is fitted with a replica of the Gemini space capsule to test ejection seats that will be used in case of a malfunction during lift-off or reentry. As the space capsule, attached to the rocket sled, reaches 550 mph, the dummies in the ejection seats are shot straight up high enough for a parachute to open and give them a safe ride back down. No astronaut goes into space without seeing the tests made by dummies first.

If $3500 seems like a high price for one anthropomorphic dummy, it is! But no one wants to put a price on the value of a human life. If only one life is saved by one dummy, the price tag is cheap. Half a million dollars go into the training of one good combat pilot and each dummy can account for many more than one pilot he has saved.

The anthropomorphic dummy comes in eight sizes. He is the VIP of the dummy world, since "anthropomorphic" means "as humanlike as possible." The slightest difference in a dummy's center of gravity can cause trouble. An ejection seat with an automatic device set to open the parachute only when the pilot—who may be unconscious—reaches a safe altitude is just one of the times that center of

Ejection starts as sled reaches 550 mph (bottom photo)

Seat rockets propel both dummies to a safe altitude (center photo)

Ride down is much slower (top photo)

NASA

79

gravity becomes important. Any slight difference might start the seat in a killer spin. This could cause the testers to reject a seat that is perfectly good, or worse—to accept one that is really faulty—all because the dummy was not perfect.

An anthropomorphic dummy also has a better memory immediately after each test than a human might. But his memory is not in his head, it's locked in his chest. There he carries up to twenty-five pounds of delicate and expensive instruments that will answer almost any question a researcher can ask. The dummy records the altitude for any given moment, his inside as well as the outside temperatures, the amount of vibration he feels, the shock impact on ejecting and on landing, the pressures on different parts of his body, the stress strain at certain points, the amount of roll and pitch and yaw; the level of sulphur dioxide and carbon dioxide in the air. Accelerometers no larger than a quarter tell how fast he traveled—up, down, forward and backward, or sideways. Load links show how much strain was put on his lap belt, shoulder harness, or even whether one side of his parachute pulled more than another. All these details are vital to know before a man himself is allowed to risk his life in tests.

Even though dummies come first every time, they are not about to replace man as a tester. Researchers think of a dummy as a tool. They find out all they can from him, but only a human can really testify to bruises,

A dummy looks over the astronauts' Mercury suits as he dresses

NASA

The dummy is ready for his testing job in the "Freedom-7" later flown by Astronaut Alan B. Shepard, Jr.

NASA

discomforts, and especially human reactions. The most perfect dummy made still cannot imitate some of the motions that seem so simple to a human—the way his head rotates on his neck or the way he can easily fling his arm up and back. Researchers could not tell

80

Suspended over the fire pit, a dummy tests a flight suit at 2200°F. temperature and is saved by the specially constructed material of his inner suit

from a dummy whether a man could remain conscious during ejection or whether he could think clearly enough to pull himself out of the dreaded killer spin that sometimes occurs before a parachute is opened.

One fact is certain—dummies are easier to find than people when they are needed. Usually they are hanging on a hook somewhere. "That's the only way we can dress them," say the testers. "A 185-pound deadweight is not the easiest thing to put clothes or shoes on." Most dummies come dressed in work overalls that unzip easily to get at the instrumentation in the chest. Dummies that take part in the space projects must have pressure-tight closings for their chests. Some are dressed

Sierra Sam has seen better days, but his experiences in the centrifuge started the astronauts on their way to the moon

OFFICIAL U.S. NAVY PHOTO

in frogmen's suits to take part in underwater tests.

A pilot can leave a burning plane only if he is wearing protective clothing. Dummies are elected to test flame retardant suits and gloves before the best material is chosen to make up thousands of uniforms. The clothing on the dummy is tested over a fuel fire pit, where it may burn only 145°F. at its center but reaches 2200°F. at its outside edges, where the oxygen helps it to burn hotter. After the dummy is swung through the fire, perhaps being exposed to it only 3.5 seconds—the time it would take a pilot to run through the flames—the dummy's body is examined carefully for signs of damage.

Safety-test dummies also have a few interchangeable parts. A special pair of hands that can grasp like a human's are important in certain tests. For example, a tractor operator's life may depend on whether or not he holds on to the wheel if the tractor rolls over. The special hands are meant to grasp up to a certain force. After that, a shear pin breaks and the hand unclasps just as it would in a human subjected to that same force.

Sierra Sam is one dummy who gets to be first almost every time. When he began work in 1956, the aerospace program was very new. No one was quite sure how a human would react to weightlessness and to whirling around in a centrifuge. Since that time, Sierra Sam's seat has been used by almost every astronaut. Sierra Sam's trips in

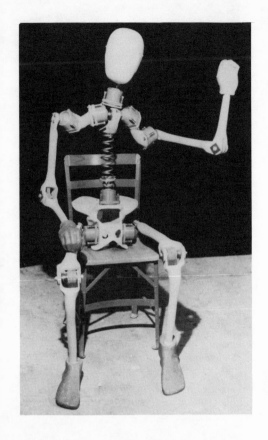

Dynamic Dan cheerfully waves before getting dressed for a drop test

Dan helps determine pilot reaction to the high forces he meets in getting out of a disabled aircraft

the centrifuge have taken him on simulated flights in the X-15, DynaSoar, Mercury, Gemini, and Apollo spacecrafts. He spent a wild day simulating a Boeing 707 swept-wing jet testing clear air turbulence and another day spinning crazily in a Navy F-4.

Dynamic Dan is called a mechanical analog. He claims to have all the mechanical characteristics found in the human body. There is not much of Dan. He looks as if he had never had a square meal, but his body has as much elasticity as a human's. His creators plan to give him a cousin who can show something that so far no dummy can show—injuries. He will have some breakable, but easily replaced, element in each part of the body where accidents occur most frequently. Dan's cousin may be just what the doctor ordered, because dummies now can test only what happens to the equipment they try out. Doctors know little about what may happen to the man the dummy substitutes for.

Automotive safety testing keeps dummies very busy today, but in 1925 the car buyer was looking only for a motor that didn't vibrate, balloon tires, a speedometer that went up to 70 mph —even though the car wouldn't go that fast—and a machine guaranteed to "ride the ruts with comfort." Within a few years, Ford Motor Company had added a safety glass windshield. The time had come to think about more safety in automobiles.

83

Another dummy that wouldn't be caught dead wearing a seat belt . . . movie camera records that unbelted driver fell on passenger as car rolled (upper left) *. . . passenger flew out side window* (lower left) *and landed 50 feet from car*

THE EDUCATIONAL AFFAIRS DEPT., FORD MOTOR CO.

Four hundred crashes a year is about average for just one of the large automobile proving grounds. Such crashes are all staged "on purpose," and the purpose is more safety for every person who rides in a car. This sort of program would take a long list of volunteers if it were not for dummies, but they were invented for just this kind of job. The day's program may include shattering a road barrier, careening off a brick wall, smashing into the rear end of another car, a collision into the side of a bus, a roll-over test on the road and another one tumbling down a steep hill. Then there is the drop test where a car is lifted by a crane and dropped 30 feet down on its nose. Unless the test is for the early stages of a car's design, these cars are all occupied by dummy "people." After a quick trip to the "hospital," where their instruments are removed and checked, the dummies are sent "home" to wait their next turn.

The same rocket sled that was used to test aircraft and spacecraft has been adapted for the automobile proving grounds. There it is called an impact sled. The new car, mounted on the sled, rides 100 feet on a rail. It is sent on its short journey by the impact of a hydropneumatic ram that can be set to start the car at any speed. Since the idea is to test various parts of the car for crash worthiness, the stop is as abrupt as the start. The dummy's job is to show how the newly designed

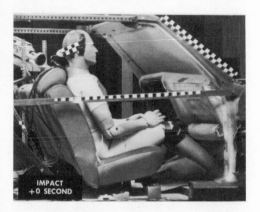
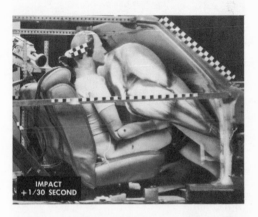

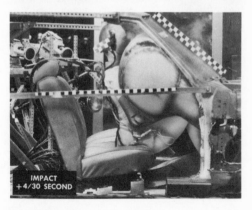

A moment before the crash on the impact sled (upper left). *Shock of collision releases compressed air into nylon safety bag* (upper right). *Dummy, without seat belt, is thrown toward windshield and hits bag* (lower left). *Dummy's weight helps deflate bag to avoid bouncing back violently* (lower right)

GENERAL MOTORS CORP.

Black-and-white markers are attached to dummy's head to aid in measuring his movements

steering wheels, seat anchors, seat belts, instrument panels, or any other features will affect a person during a crash. There are many ways to design features so that they will be attractive, but the automobile companies will choose only those which are the safest. The new designs that tested best on the impact sled are then tried with outdoor crashes on the proving grounds.

The anthropomorphic dummies that work in automobiles are a special breed. Unlike some of their anthropomorphic buddies, these must have a full range of human responses. For example, when the body jackknifes in an accident, the human spine stretches out a couple of inches from its normal sitting position. The dummy's spine is made so this will happen to him just as it would to a person. Some have for a forehead a piece of foam that will retain a hard bump mark after the dummy strikes the windshield or dashboard in an accident. The dummy, however, cannot indicate yet whether a real person would have suffered brain damage from such an accident. Since most of the car-testing dummy's work is done sitting down, his makers have copied the human pelvis to make him sit right. His hip sockets and pelvic bones are modeled directly from human bones. Dummies were originally all made to stand up, so they could not sit down properly unless their legs had chunks of "flesh" cut out to make the torso sit straight like a human's. For tests where a dummy must stand, such as testing the safety of a passenger riding a bus standing up and holding onto the strap overhead, he will have a back stiffener added as well as one of the special "grasping hands."

Dummies can take the credit for discovering the second collision. When an accident occurs between two cars or a car and an immovable object, there is a collision. The passengers might often get out and walk away if it were not for that second collision, the one taking place between the occupants of the car and the various parts inside the car that they collide against. Slow-motion movie cameras recording the action inside and outside test crashes help the researchers to see exactly where and how this second collision happens. Seat belts and shoulder harnesses were invented because of it.

Ten thousand people will die this year because they did not use their seat belts. Usually these are the older folks who are not used to them. They forget to put them on and complain that the belts muss their clothes. But actually they do not really understand the reason the seat belts are there. People who don't use seat belts are just like the old World War I pilots who could have used parachutes, but didn't bother.

Young people are much more likely to use seat belts, because they under-stand—as many older people do not —that automobiles are designed to "crush." Instead of being built tougher up front, where most impacts occur, the cars are designed to crush in a controlled way that keeps the damage far in front of the passenger compartment. The controlled crush absorbs some of the force, just as Isaac Newton said it would long before anyone thought of inventing an automobile. It is like hitting a haystack and not getting hurt as much as by hitting a concrete wall, even though the car is traveling just as fast. Unfortunately, this improvement is not going to help at all the person who fails to use his seat belt.

Sophisticated Sam helps auto manu-

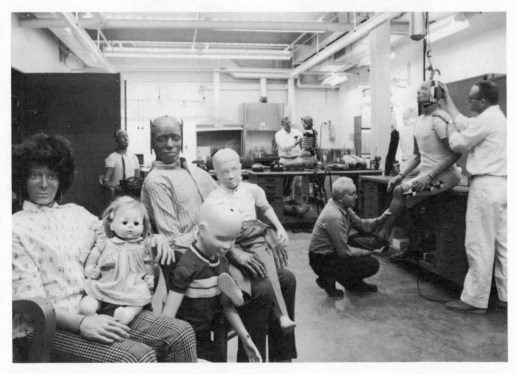

A dummy family wait their turn in the "hospital"

GENERAL MOTORS CORP.

facturers to find out how badly an accident may affect a passenger. He even has bones that will break. If his head hits the dashboard, he may break his nose. Then the dashboard goes back to the drawing board for a new design or for some energy-absorbing padding to make it safer.

Sophisticated Sam usually tests with a seat belt and shoulder harness on. Even a dummy wouldn't be caught dead not wearing them.

None of the dummies "survived" this accident staged without seat belts
NATIONAL SAFETY COUNCIL

9

What a "Hot" Dummy Does

RADIANT MODELS

NOT ALL THE DANGER dummies are subjected to is violent. One of the most dangerous forces known to man is radiation. Astronauts face an unknown amount of radiation in space. No one is quite sure whether passengers in supersonic transports may also be exposed to radiation—especially the crew members who will be making many trips in the superhigh altitudes.

Before the bomb was dropped on Hiroshima and Nagasaki in 1945, few Americans knew much about radiation. Soon they began learning exactly what had happened in those two Japanese cities and knew that no country would ever again be free from that fear.

Less than ten years later, the fear had grown so much that many people built themselves underground bomb shelters. No one really knew either whether their shelters would work. It was time to learn exactly how much damage exposure to radiation might do and how a person could protect himself and his family from radiation damage. Operation Doorstep was planned by three groups, the Atomic Energy Commission, the Department of Defense, and the Federal Civil Defense Administration. They also wanted to know what would happen if an atomic bomb ever dropped on their doorstep.

A bomb target was set up in Nevada, where some test bombing had already been done. Two houses, typical of those found anywhere in the United States, were built. One was less than a mile from the bomb and the other was just over a mile away. Since the amount of money allowed for the experiment was too small to build more than two houses, elaborate precautions were taken to make sure those two were not destroyed by fire. Both houses had basement shelters. Eight different types of outdoor bomb shelters were also built at varying distances from the target center. Several types of passenger cars were scattered through the area. When all was ready, the bomb was placed atop a 300-foot tower.

Then dummy families were moved in. Some stayed in the basement shelters. Some were having a dinner party in the dining rooms of both houses. One was in bed on the second floor. Others sat in the living room waiting for the blast.

Instruments were set up to record the effect. Film badges were placed in one hundred spots in each basement to record radiation there. Movie cameras were positioned to record any action in slow motion. Three . . . two . . . one . . . *zero!*

At that instant and for a minute afterward, the initial radiation filled the air. The houses were charred, but there was no fire. Then the radioactive matter slowly rose into the bomb cloud —to return again in the form of fallout. A split second after the thermal wave came the blast wave. It was the blast wave that blew out the windows, carrying flying glass and metal like thousands of daggers. Some of the walls collapsed, especially in the house nearest the bomb.

The initial radiation, which lasted a minute after the thermal wave, was the most dangerous for the manikins. Unfortunately, however, a change in wind carried the fallout to where the automobiles were parked and to the houses. For this reason, film badges could not be recovered until they had collected thirty hours of fallout radiation as well as the initial radiation.

When it was safe enough for the Civil Defense teams to take a closer look, here is what they found: The mannequins living less than a mile from ground zero had a hard time. Those in the living room were covered with debris and those in the dining room were buried under rubble. Had they been humans, they would have received severe initial radiation burns. But down in the basement, in a crude lean-to type of shelter, sat one of the mannequins. Although parts of the first floor had caved in around her shelter, not a hair of her fancy hairdo was disturbed.

The family living farther away from the blast center was in better shape. Those in the living room had been toppled about. One man sat almost as he had before the blast, but pieces of flying glass had chipped his plaster eyes. The dinner party had ended abruptly with the windows flying onto the table. Upstairs a mannequin lay in bed. All the bedclothes had been blown off by the blast, and a trail of overturned furniture showed where the blast had torn through the room. This mannequin, as well as the others, did

This family just moved in—for a short stay

not suffer much from radiation. They all could have received bad burns from the thermal wave, however. The happiest-looking group in this house was the family in the basement shelter. They had been completely protected from initial radiation, but if it had taken several hours before they were rescued, they would have had radiation sickness from fallout.

The mannequins staying in outside underground shelters, however, survived the best—mainly because they were safe from fire. The houses were carefully fireproofed so that they would not go up in flames, taking valuable information with them, but in a real emergency typical houses would probably have burned. For that reason, Civil Defense workers warned people building shelters in or near their houses to prepare extra escape routes, because of the great danger of fire.

A lady dummy appears unconcerned about the totally destroyed house that has collapsed into her basement shelter

Radiation is a new force to be reckoned with. Following Operation Doorstep, the Atomic Energy Commission set up regulations governing how much exposure to radiation is safe for persons working with it continually. Booklets were published to advise families how to build or make the safest kinds of shelters, what foods to store in them, and how to best prepare for such an emergency.

Most problems with radiation are not so dramatic. It is good to know that the same radiation that can cause death and destruction can also cure people who might otherwise die of cancer or can be used to take X-ray photographs of persons who are sick from unknown causes. But anything that exposes a human being to radiation is very dangerous and learning to use radiation properly is a dangerous occupation.

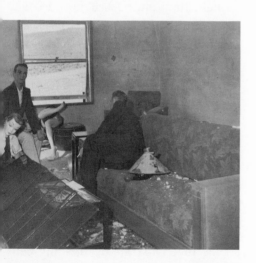

Zero hour hits the dummy family near an atomic blast

The Phantom Patient has a real human skeleton molded in plastic, which makes him unique in the dummy world. Following close on the heels of the discovery of the X-ray machine was the disappointing news that X-rays were very dangerous and could build up radiation in the human body. Here was this marvelous invention—the X-ray machine—but how were technicians going to learn to use it? Worse yet, doctors had radioactive medicines that might cure a hopeless case of cancer, but how were they going to learn how to give them to their patients?

In addition to his skeleton, the Phantom Patient needed organs that would photograph in the X-ray machine. What would be the soft tissues in a human are a medium-hard rubber

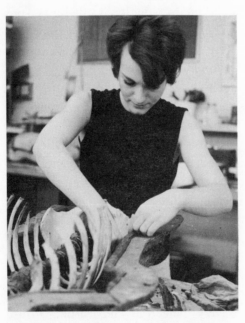

A human skeleton is packed inside the Phantom Patient's tough plastic form

in the Phantom Patient. But they photograph just like the real thing after they are filled with water through a convenient opening in the top of his head. A small amount of fungicide must be added to the water or else organisms will start growing in the bones. Some of the organs, like the stomach, gall bladder, and bladder, can be filled with another liquid that will make them stand out in contrast in X-ray photographs. Filled with water, the same organs will not show up on X-rays. A pump forces fluid through the Phantom Patient's arteries at 72 beats a minute. To be completely cooperative, he comes apart so students can concentrate their study on any one particular part of his body.

The Phantom Patient trains radiologists, because they are the people who diagnose and treat diseases in patients by using radioactive substances. First though, they must learn how to take sharp X-ray pictures of the bones and organs before they can spot tumors and other suspicious growths. The actual detection of tumors, they can learn by studying X-rays of people who already have growths. Without the Phantom Patient, the radiologist could not learn how to use the techniques and machinery he must work with.

Once a patient is found to have a tumor, the radiotherapist can bombard the growth with a radioactive substance that kills rapidly dividing cells such as cancer cells. But it is not so easy as all that. The body has other rapidly dividing cells, in the intestines, for instance, that are good cells and cannot be destroyed. When the beam of radiation is aimed toward the one bad spot, it will also pass through the patient's skin, tissues, and other organs that are perfectly healthy. What will happen to the healthy parts of the body while the beam is treating the one unhealthy spot? And for how long a time should the beam be trained on the cancerous growth? How much is too much? And how deeply should the beam penetrate to get into the growth, but not go right on through it?

Rando, the dummy, came along to answer these riddles. In order to avoid harming the healthy tissues and organs, the radioactive beam is focused on the cancerous growth. Then it is aimed on that same spot from several different angles. This way the beam passes through healthy tissues only once, but through the growth every time. Rando is given a test treatment and all the errors adjusted so there will be no mistakes when the human patient is treated.

Rando comes in two sizes—the average man or the average woman. He/ she is made with a human skeleton molded into a rubber mold. The body duplicates a human body as closely as possible, but since movement is not at all important, none is provided for. Rando does not even have arms and legs. But the lungs, soft tissues, and air spaces are all there, along with the skeleton. What makes Rando unusual among dummies is that he comes in slices like a loaf of bread! Each one-inch thick slice has holes in it and, through these holes, the amount of radiation is measured. He absorbs radiation just as the human body would, but the radiologist can learn how much radiation is being received by each portion of Rando's body—something he could never learn from the human patient. Rando takes all the chances and the human patient gets all the benefits!

As scientists became more concerned with the amount of radiation astronauts may get in space, they began wishing they had someone like the Phantom Patient around. But astro-

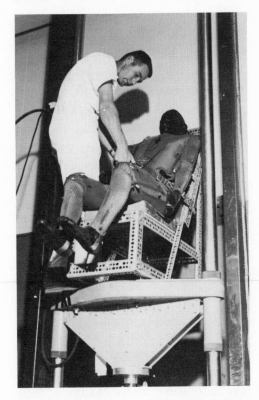

The Plastinaut gets set for a high G-force test

nauts take quite a bit of banging around, and just the matter of taking off in a space capsule was too much for the Phantom Patient. The job was open, and the Plastinaut came to fill it.

There was no way to find out what the radiation hazards are and how to protect astronauts and crewmen of supersonic transports from them without sending some sort of manikin into space. The Plastinaut wears a nylon suit that holds him tightly together, although he is also made with a human skeleton molded in rubber. He can accelerate up to 40G's. Once out in space, his body absorbs radiation and high-energy protons just as a human would. But unlike a human, the radiation the Plastinaut absorbs can be measured. As space travel pushes farther out, his job may become much more dangerous. Spacecraft now stay under the 300-mile-up limit to orbit. If they did not, they could enter the Van Allen radiation belts, where the spaceship crew would receive enough radiation to die within a few hours. Blast-offs and landings for interplanetary travel will probably be in the polar regions in order to avoid the Van Allen radiation belts. If so, some Plastinauts will no doubt be needed to test that new route of escape from planet Earth.

Remcal and Remab are phantoms with highly specialized jobs. Both are anthropomorphic. They are as human-like as possible and in addition, their bodies have the same reactions to radiation as a human body. But there

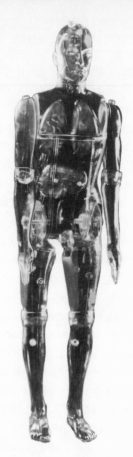

Remcal takes the patient's radioactive dose first to make sure it's the right amount
ALDERSON RESEARCH LABORATORIES, INC.

the similarity ends. Before a doctor can treat a cancerous growth or even be certain how and where the growth is and what other body functions the growth may be interfering with, he must measure it carefully by machines designed for that purpose. An X-ray only shows there is something there. Other machines take over from that point.

Remcal's body is of clear plastic. He has no skeleton, but he does have all the organs that might be treated by radioisotopes. He even has "tumors" that can be made to order. When the radioisotopes are placed in his body, a radiotherapist is able to probe into Remcal to measure the dosage at any point he chooses—something he may wish to do with a human patient but could not possibly try. Remcal is very helpful in setting up the machines that will measure the human patient. If a doctor needs to study the liver function in his real patient, he uses Remcal's liver to calibrate the instrument. Then the instrument is ready to measure the sick patient's liver function.

Remab also has a clear plastic skin, but inside it he has a human skeleton. His bones have been carefully sealed to prevent any absorbing of the radio-isotopes he works with, because Remab's chief characteristic is that he is an absorber. What makes him so popular with doctors is his willingness to let them know exactly how much radiation he has absorbed. A human patient gives almost no feedback information on how much radiation he may have absorbed in different parts of his body. Remab can be probed at any point to see how much radiation has gone into his kidneys, tissues, stomach.

A workman at a nuclear waste disposal site has backed his bulldozer accidentally over a sealed container. Without thinking, he jumps down from his seat to go behind the bulldozer and see what he has hit. When he sees it was a sealed container, he tries for a few minutes to cover it over. Then a glance at the dosimeter he carries tells him that he has already received

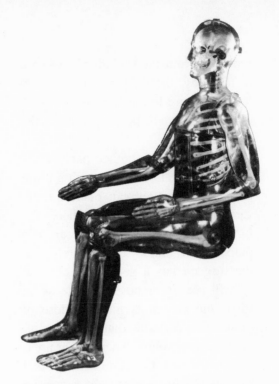

Remab lets the doctor know what goes on inside a human patient

ALDERSON RESEARCH LABORATORIES, INC.

a serious dose of radiation. He has been on the job long enough to know the danger of his situation. He reports the accident so that men wearing more protective clothing can get rid of the nuclear material that is seeping out of the container. But he is rushed off to the hospital. The doctors use what knowledge they have of treating radiation damage, but mostly now it will be a matter of treating each serious symptom as it shows up—perhaps a day or a week from now. That is all they can do. Or is that all?

Remab is called in. He is given the same type of radiation exposure that the workman had. Now Remab's body can be tested at any one point and before the workman can develop serious reactions from the radiation anywhere in his body, the doctors can be ready for it, because Remab's body could indicate what might be happening in the workman.

Meanwhile, in another part of the hospital, there is a patient with a brain tumor. Before they can operate, doctors must know exactly where the tumor is. The Head Phantom can help pinpoint the tumor so accurately that the surgeon has a good idea of what he will see when he opens the skull. First, the patient is given a dose of radioactive material that concentrates in the brain tumor. Then his brain is "scanned" and the radioactivity that has entered the cancer cells shows up on the scanner and forms a "picture" of the tumor. Now it is time for the Head Phantom. Rods enter his skull, which is encased in plastic. Small hollow plastic ends of the rods are filled with a measured amount of radioactive material. These plastic spheres represent the tumor inside the Head Phantom, matching the real patient's tumor. The brain scan of the Head Phantom is made and the "tumor" is moved around inside the skull until his brain

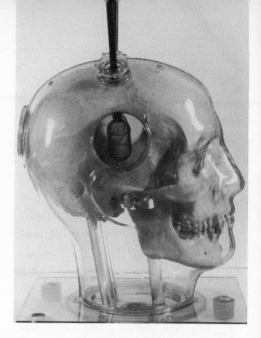

The Head Phantom's movable tumors are connected to rods that go through his skull
ALDERSON RESEARCH LABORATORIES, INC.

scan exactly duplicates the scan of the patient's head. When the two brain scans match, the Head Phantom can be said to have a tumor just like the patient's—with one difference. The doctor can see the tumor in the Head Phantom and now he can "see" what is going on inside his own patient's head almost as if he had X-ray eyes.

Dummies are the ideal recruits when medicine wages all-out nuclear war on diseases such as cancer.

10

Dummies for Fun and Learning
DUMMY GAMES

TWO POLICE SQUAD CARS came to an abrupt stop in front of a Florida office recently. Passersby stopped and gaped as a big policeman strode purposefully inside. Someone ill? Robbery? What could have happened? The crowd pressed closer to the large window.

Inside, the policeman was waving a citation and pointing toward a parrot outside in a cage. Soon the owner and the policeman came out to where a second policeman was talking to the parrot.

"The Humane Society was started just because of people like you," the first policeman was saying. "This poor parrot is even fading in this broiling sun."

"Look, chief, there isn't even a dish of water in the cage—just like the lady who filed the complaint said. You oughta be ashamed," said the other policeman.

It was not until the owner showed them the tape recorder inside the parrot's stomach that either of the policemen believed the bird was a dummy.

As for the lady who had called the Humane Society, she still stops occasionally to see if there is water in the cage.

Dummies do not often get the chance to mimic great people, especially with any real accuracy. For two summers, Abraham Lincoln lived again in New York City at the World's Fair of 1964–1965. When Walt Disney planned to re-create Lincoln, all the biographies of the great man were turned inside out to find mannerisms and characteristics that were true of Lincoln alone. The face for the dummy Lincoln was modeled from a mask made during Lincoln's lifetime. The dummy's schedule was not an easy one —five times an hour he rose from his chair to greet audiences and quote some of Lincoln's best-known words. But what made him really alive was the expressions and the gestures that were known to be Lincoln's alone. The dummy had a repertoire of 250,000 possible combinations he could use for his impersonation!

Charlie plays a mechanical piano in

a Florida restaurant. He usually fills in for the "live" entertainers while they are on break. The live ones get tired and thirsty. The singers have to rest their voices, and the musicians can play only a certain number of minutes during the hour, because they belong to a union. None of these problems bothers Charlie. He would just as soon play his Gay Nineties tunes all day and all night if they would let him. He doesn't even take time out to flirt with the waitresses.

Recently, though, someone thought Charlie was looking a little seedy. His managers decided he ought to get a checkup and have a little change of scenery—and maybe get a clean collar. So Charlie rode over 250 miles in a bus seat to get a retouch job from his creators. Then back to the job again, with another load of passengers wondering who that odd character was in the front seat. The bus driver called Charlie a model passenger.

Not all dummies that work for the automobile industry lead thrill-packed lives testing cars. Some of them help design "next year's model." A 2-D dummy is much like the paper people that children make in grade school, with movable arms and legs attached to the body by means of a paper fastener. Before a new car gets off the drawing board is the best time to find out whether it will seat people comfortably. The designer fits the 2-D manikin into his newly drawn seat to check whether he can reach the floor comfortably, sit up without bumping

Charlie, the honky-tonk piano player, is joined by a hurdy-gurdy man and a talkative parrot

ANIMATED DISPLAY CREATORS, INC.

his head on the roof, and have enough legroom so he won't get a charley horse from being cramped in the back seat.

After the design of the new car is approved, a prototype is made. To all appearances, this is the "new" car, but there will still be many more changes made. The manikin used to check this car for comfort does not even have to look like a person. One dummy consists of a "back pan" that rests against the car back and a "seat pan" that it sits on. It has two metal "legs" that can be adjusted for length to reach the gas and brake pedals. Instead of a head, it has a sliding vertical tube that is called a headroom probe. Weights are added after the dummy is sitting in the seat so its weight will be equivalent to a human's. This kind of manikin is easy to try in all the car's seats and can be moved easily.

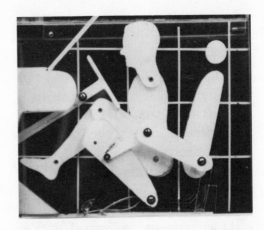

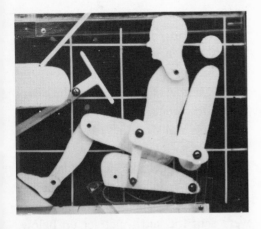

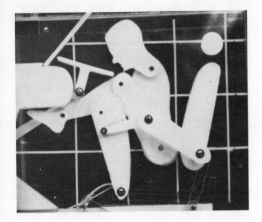

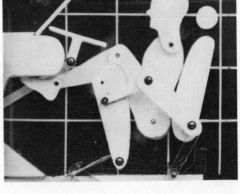

Two-dimensional model of a protective seat shows dummy in normal position without a seat belt

0.040 seconds after a simulated impact at 15G, the cushion has lifted to catch dummy's center of gravity

0.080 seconds after impact, powered by rubber bands, the dummy starts to rebound

0.120 seconds after impact, the dummy safely settles back against the back of the protective seat

OFFICIAL PHOTOS: U.S. NAVY

Even though he looks as if he had lost his head somewhere, the car-designing manikin has an important job. When people buy a car, they look for many different kinds of comfort. Can they sit in the car with a hat on? Can all the pedals be reached by most drivers, or only by the long-legged ones? Will short teen-agers be able to see over the wheel by the time they get their learners' permits? After the seat belt is fastened, can the driver still open the window when he reaches a turnpike toll booth? When the front seat is pulled forward for a teen-age driver to reach the pedals, will the other front seat passenger get his knees squashed by the glove compartment? In the rush to build new cars that look different from last year's model, auto manufacturers often don't ask the manikin enough questions. Even a dummy can tell them where they have made some mistakes.

Dummies did not become overnight successes in Hollywood. In the earliest days of silent movies, when the script called for the villain to go over a cliff, the director first tried to find a stunt man who would bounce painfully down the cliff to lie sprawled hundreds of feet below. If the extra five dollars in the weekly paycheck was not enough to entice a stunt man to do the job, the director reluctantly called for a dummy. But the dummy usually looked like a suit of long underwear stuffed with straw, which is exactly what it was.

Early movie audiences had paid their nickels and dimes for an afternoon of thrills and they got them. When a pale movie starlet splashed in the ocean with a look of helpless terror on her face, she was not acting. Chances were good that, until that very day, the starlet had not known that her role required her to be saved from a watery death or she might have mentioned that she couldn't swim. The director would not have cared anyway. He knew the cameraman would catch her panic-stricken splashing on the film and someone could jump in and save her

after the scene was made. No audience was going to pay fifteen cents or even twenty-five cents to see a dummy drowning!

The battle of Babylon in the silent epic *Intolerance* was becoming a problem. The walls of the city were over ninety feet high, but how was the audience to get the feeling of such spectacular height unless a few bodies were thrown off the walls? Stunt men were sent for and a net set up below. But only one of the stunt men knew how to land in the net without bouncing back up into the camera range as though he were on a trampoline.

"Don't land on your feet," he warned the others. He jumped first to show how it was done. But the next three men all landed feet first, doubled over, and broke their noses.

Reluctantly D. W. Griffith, the director, called for the dummies. They had already been used in some long shots but were far enough away from the camera to look convincing. Close up it was painfully obvious the way they flopped around that they were not real people. Joseph Henabery, an actor and Griffith's best helper, had an idea. Taking the dummies, he fastened thin string to the arms and legs. When each dummy landed, the strings would snap—one at a time—and an arm or leg would fly loose. The effect looked realistic enough. The only problem now was that each dummy had to be restrung for every fall.

Most of the daring stunts were done for comedies, but often dummies got the last laugh. Harold Lloyd liked doing his own stunts, even though he had lost a thumb and forefinger while having his picture taken holding what was supposed to be a fake bomb. He is remembered as the mild young man with large spectacles who somehow always wound up on the outside rim of a building several floors up from the street. Sometimes his sets were built on the roof of a building to get the effect of height without having to hang out over the street to get it. Workmen built him a platform just in case Lloyd, who insisted on doing his own stunts even with only one hand, might slip. After the filming of the show was over, his fellow workers got around to wondering whether the wooden platform would have caught him anyway. One of them dropped a dummy from the spot where Lloyd had worked that day. The dummy bounced once on the catwalk and then dropped down into the street. Moviemaking was too dangerous a sport for dummies.

In *Manslaughter*, the heroine was a speed demon. In one scene, her car was to be chased by a motorcycle policeman. Then her car was to skid around and be hit dead center by the motorcycle. The stunt man earned his extra five dollars that day. As the motorcycle struck the car right on cue, the stunt man somersaulted over the car landing on the other side with broken ribs, pelvis, and collarbone. Later the actress commented, "They shouldn't have risked a man's life for that shot. When you see it on the screen, it looks exactly like a dummy!"

Hollywood movie directors relied on the luck and good sense of their stunt men too often. As the directors thought up bigger and better thrills to keep audiences pouring into movie houses, the accidents began piling up. The sort of action that attracted people involved swinging down a ladder from an airplane to a moving train, climbing from one plane to another, jumping off a moving train onto an overhead wire, canoeing down a rampaging rapids. Where action used to mean Douglas Fairbanks leaping out of a window to land on a horse two stories below, action now meant doing the same thing, only landing on a motorcycle.

Audiences were becoming almost immune to the cliff-hanger ending of each serial episode. They knew now that the hero and heroine would be miraculously saved at the beginning of the next episode and in another hopeless mess by the end of it. It was getting harder and harder to make thrillers thrilling. The director of the first *Ben-Hur* carried the use of real people instead of dummies to a fatal extreme. Dozens of horses were killed during the filming of the chariot race. Six, in one day! But it was the fiery clash between the slave ship and the pirate ship that really upset newspapers and public opinion. When the Italian extras had been hired for that particular scene, which was filmed in Italy, each had been asked whether he could swim. A simple "Yes" answer got a job paying each peasant more money than he

Will Sell does not always have his mind on business

could ever make in the fields. To make sure one of the ships would burn well, it had been liberally doused with oil—without warning the passengers. No one ever combed through all the conflicting stories of the filming enough to prove how many extras were drowned that day! Instead of appreciating the fact that people were giving their lives for entertainment, fickle movie audiences decided about then that they preferred good stories to thrills after all. Today dummies, looking much more real, still take on the most dangerous jobs, to prevent tragedy.

Sometimes dummies get the last word. Will Sell has one of the most enviable wardrobes in dummyland. For his job as a salesman he has several business suits, sports coats, and shirts.

When men wear wide neckties, so does Will. When white shirts are out and blue shirts are in, he follows the trend. He has a pixie suit and cowboy clothes for children's shows, overalls to go to county fairs, a cap and gown for educational conventions, a football uniform for sports shows, and a sweater with a big "Y" for Y.M.C.A. or Y.M.H.A. conferences. He was even seen wearing a striped prison uniform, behind a fence made of cigarettes, and said he was a "prisoner of the smoking habit." Will's mouth is coordinated to move with a tape-recorded voice, but sometimes a live speaker, hiding behind a two-way glass mirror, speaks through him.

Ed has a job with NASA testing the microphones and earphones that go into the astronaut's helmets. He is an electronic dummy. When Ed speaks, he tests the microphone through which an astronaut can be heard all over the world—"One small step for man. . . ." Ed didn't think up those words, but the microphone he tested worked successfully, or the world would never have heard them spoken from the moon.

Ed's ear is as sensitive to noise as a human's. Although his ears cannot be hurt by prolonged loud noises like a human ear, he will be used to evaluate human reactions to noise. When an astronaut puts on his earphones, he can be sure that Ed tested them first.

Some dummies work at miniature golf courses, where the day's—and night's—work is to distract the golf

102

player from making a perfect shot, with such diversions as a mechanical hula. Many more work in amusement parks, where plenty of jobs are available in the right season. Monsters, the uglier the better, can always get a job at the thrill rides. Cannibals and gorillas find work in fake jungles and an animated skeleton is never unemployed so long as there is a haunted house.

Working in Disneyland is to a dummy what getting in a Broadway show is to an actor, or what being elected President might be to a Senate page boy. It's the top of the ladder. Disneyland dummies are an exclusive lot, because they are all Disney creations. The inner workings of the special audio-animatronic animals are secrets, but these very special dummies that speak and move will perform for any child who can visit either the Disneyland in California or the newer Disneyland East, in Florida.

Laura Dale is one dummy who really likes to play games. Actually, she is a combination doll and psychologist and microwave radio. Her entire day is spent playing with children. The children, however, are mentally retarded and among the fifty boys and girls she plays with in a day, only a few can speak an entire sentence. The strange fact is that many of those children will speak to Laura Dale. They will tell her their names. When Laura Dale tells them her name and says "I like you," the conversation may go on and on.

Of course, the voice of Laura Dale

is really a therapist talking through an electronic transmitter. There are no wires connecting the doll to the transmitter, so the child is not suspicious that an adult is talking back to her. "Can you say hello?" Laura Dale asks sweetly, and the child answers, "Hello." It's a beginning. The same retarded child would not say a single word to any adult or to another child. And there is no way this child can be helped unless she can be taught to communicate and relate to other children.

One of Laura Dale's talents is that she can speak any language in the

Passengers boarding the "Flight to the Moon" in Disneyland pass through this moon mission control center manned by audio-animatronic scientists

world. There are about twenty like her in the United States, and other countries are hoping soon to have Laura Dales of their own.

Meanwhile Snoopy has left his doghouse to see what can be done for the thousands of deaf children—most of them victims of German measles epidemics. Snoopy talks and listens through a transmitter and receiver implanted in his body. The teacher, in another room, is really Snoopy's voice and ears. The sound reaches the children through bone conduction when they press their ears against the dog. Fortunately Snoopy sits about four feet tall, so there is space for plenty of ears to press against his soft side. Because children respond better to Snoopy than to an adult, he makes it easier for a speech therapist to diagnose and treat each child's individual hearing problem.

It's smart to use a dummy—especially when a dummy can do something better than a human can!

BIOGRAPHY OF SUZANNE HILTON

Suzanne Hilton has too much curiosity and that is why she began writing books.

She was born in Pittsburgh, Pennsylvania, but a family pattern of moving often into strange new neighborhoods started an inquisitiveness that has never been curbed. She attended nearly a dozen schools from California to Pennsylvania before attending Pennsylvania College for Women (now Chatham College) in Pittsburgh and graduating from Beaver College in Glenside, Pennsylvania.

During World War II she used her knowledge of languages as a volunteer in the Foreign Inquiry Department of the American Red Cross. After the war, she married Warren M. Hilton, now an industrial and insurance engineer and Lt. Colonel, U. S. Army Reserve. With their son, Bruce, and daughter, Diana, the Hiltons traveled thousands of miles camping and sailing. There was always that insatiable curiosity—to see what might be around the next curve.

"Libraries were always luring me," she says when asked how she likes researching for a book. "Researching is like having a mystery to solve. I know that the answer I'm digging for is hidden somewhere in all those books and the search is so exciting I can forget to eat."

But researching about dummies involved more than just libraries. The fun part was meeting the dummies.

"I had no idea that dummies could have such personalities. I never met one that didn't have a name," says Mrs. Hilton. "Each had a special dignity, but each also shared some sort of joke with the humans he worked with. The big boss at one testing ground had found a dummy in his chair one morning, with his feet on the desk and the boss's cigar in his hand. Another named Sam had just played a joke on the cleaning lady the night before. When she entered an office at three A.M. to clean, she nearly fainted when she saw legs sticking out from under one of the desks."

A free-lance writer and author of two previous books, Mrs. Hilton is still leading herself and her readers into strange corners of a technological world.

BIBLIOGRAPHY

The following books provided background information for various chapters.

Bell, Whitfield J., Jr., *et al., A Cabinet of Curiosities*. The University Press of Virginia, 1967.

Benkard, Ernst, *Undying Faces*. London: Hogarth Press, Ltd., 1929.

Brings, Lawrence M. (ed.), *Outdoor Horizons*. T. S. Denison & Company, 1957.

Brownlow, Kevin, *The Parade's Gone By*. Alfred A. Knopf, Inc., 1968.

Caidin, Martin, *The Silken Angels, A History of Parachuting*. J. B. Lippincott Company, 1964.

Chavasse, Pye Henry, *Advice to a Wife and Mother*. George Routledge and Sons, 1873.

Connett, Eugene V. (ed.), *Duck Shooting Along the Atlantic Tidewater*. William Morrow and Company, Inc., 1947.

Earnest, Adele, *The Art of the Decoy: American Bird Carvings*. Clarkson N. Potter, Inc., 1965.

Ehrlich, Blake, *London on the Thames*. Little, Brown and Co., 1966.

Flagg, P. J., *The Art of Resuscitation*. Reinhold Publishing Corporation, 1944.

Fraser, Antonia, *A History of Toys*. Delacorte Press Book. The Dial Press, Inc., 1966.

Goodman, Louis S., and Gilman, Alfred, *The Pharmacological Basis of Therapeutics,* 4th edition. The Macmillan Company, 1970.

Gottlieb, Leon S., *A History of Respiration*. Charles C Thomas Publisher, 1964.

Gurney, Gene, *The Smithsonian Institution*. Crown Publishers, Inc., 1964.

Guyton, Arthur C., M.D., *Textbook of Medical Physiology*. W. B. Saunders Company, 1968.

Inglis, Brian, *A History of Medicine*. The World Publishing Company, 1965.

Katz, Herbert, and Marjorie, *Museums, U.S.A.: A History and Guide*. Doubleday & Company, Inc., 1965.

Kay, James P., *The Physiology, Pathology and Treatment of Asphyxia*. London, 1834.

Mechey, William J., Jr., *American Bird Decoys*. E. P. Dutton & Company, Inc., 1965.

Meyers, Bernard S., and Shirley D. (eds.), *McGraw-Hill Dictionary of Art.* McGraw-Hill Book Company, Inc., 1969.

A New and Complete Dictionary of Arts and Sciences, by A Society of Gentlemen, Volume IV. London: Printed for W. Owen at Homer's Head in Fleet Street, 1755.

Pearson, John W., *Historical and Experimental Approaches to Modern Resuscitation.* Charles C Thomas Publisher, 1965.

Reilly, D. R., *Portrait Waxes, An Introduction for Collectors.* London: B. T. Batsford, Ltd., 1953.

Riesman, David, *The Story of Medicine in the Middle Ages.* Paul B. Hoeber, Inc., 1935.

Ripley, Dillon, *The Sacred Grove.* Simon and Schuster, Inc., 1969.

Sarton, George, *A History of Science.* John Wiley & Sons, Inc., 1959.

Schwartz, Alvin, *Museum, The Story of America's Treasure Houses.* E. P. Dutton & Company, Inc., 1967.

Sellers, Charles Coleman, *Charles Willson Peale, A Biography.* Charles Scribner's Sons, 1969.

Singer, Charles, and Underwood, E. Ashworth, *A Short History of Medicine,* Revised and Enlarged Edition. Oxford University Press, 1962.

Stedman's Medical Dictionary, 21st edition. The Williams & Wilkins Company, 1966.

Thorwald, Jurgen, *Science and Secrets of Early Medicine.* Harcourt, Brace & World, Inc., 1962.

Wendt, Lloyd, and Kogan, Herman, *Give the Lady What She Wants.* Rand McNally & Company, 1952.

Wintrobe, Maxwell N. *et al.* (eds.), *Harrison's Principles of Internal Medicine,* 6th edition. A Blakiston Publication. McGraw-Hill Book Company, Inc., 1970.

In addition to books, the following magazines, journals, and pamphlets supplied information.

Aerospace Medicine, "Current Concepts and Practices Applicable to the Control of Body Heat Loss in Aircrew Subjected to Water Immersion," Beckman, Reeves, and Goldman, April, 1963.

Aerospace Medicine, "Wet Versus Dry Suit Approaches to Water Immersion Protective Clothing," Goldman, Breckenridge, Reeves, and Beckman, May, 1966.

American Journal of Roentgenology, "Phantoms," April, 1968.

Anaesthesia, "Training Model for Intubation of Infants," April, 1968.

Archives of Ophthalmology, "Mannequin for Practice Techniques," October, 1969.

Datamation, "The Model Patient," August, 1968.

Fortune, Article on Window Display, January, 1937.

Full-Scale Dynamic Crash Test of a Douglas DC-7 Aircraft, Technical Report ADS-37, for Federal Aviation Agency, Aircraft Development Service, April, 1965. Prepared by Aviation Safety Engineering & Research Division of Flight Safety Foundation, Inc., Phoenix, Arizona.

Game Trails, Jonas Brothers, Inc., Denver, Colorado, 1970.

Health Physics, "Dose Distribution in Phantoms," December, 1968.

Industrial Research, "Getting Rid of Seat Belts," October, 1968.

Journal of Dental Education, "Dental Phantom," December, 1968.

Journal of Medical Education, "Effectiveness of a Simulator in Training Anesthesiology Residents," by Abrahamson, Denson, and Wolf, June, 1969.

Journal of Nuclear Medicine, "Human Organ Phantoms," June, 1968, and Brain Scan Phantoms," September, 1967.

Military Medicine, "Physiological Costs of Body Armor," Ralph F. Goldman, March, 1969.

The New York Times articles, 1965–1971.

Radiology, "Shaping the Dose Through a Tumor Model," Basil S. Proimos, and "The Patient Equivalence of the Rando Phantom for Cobalt Gamma Rays," W. L. Saylor and Betty L. Adams, January, 1969.

Taxidermists Supplies, Jonas Brothers, Inc., Denver, Colorado, 1970.

Time magazine articles, 1969–1971.

Eventually the time arrives when the author can find no more information in books and libraries. Here are some of the people and companies that helped then with up-to-the-minute information and photographs.

Mr. Wes Gordeuk, Connecticut

Dr. Nobuhiko Ishizuka, Tokyo, Japan

The Academy of Natural Sciences, Philadelphia

Aerojet-General Corporation

Aerospace Audio-Visual Service, U.S. Air Force

Aerospace Crew Equipment Department, U.S. Navy

Aerospace Medical Research Laboratories, U.S. Navy

Alderson Research Laboratories, Inc.

American Wax Museum, Philadelphia

Animated Display Creators, Inc.

Bell Telephone Company of Pennsylvania

Charleston Library Society Museum

M. J. Chase Co., Inc.

Dallas Health & Science Museum

Decter Mannikin Company, Inc.

Denoyer-Geppert Company

Drexel University

Dynamic Science, Arizona

Ford Motor Company

The Franklin Institute, Philadelphia

General Motors Corporation Proving Ground

Greneker Division of the Marmon Group, Inc.

Hahnemann Medical College and Hospital

Jefferson Medical College, Thomas Jefferson University

John Wanamaker, Philadelphia

Jonas Bros., Inc., Denver

Laerdal Medical Corporation

Material Engineering Section, U.S. Navy

M. J. Hofmann Company

Movieland Wax Museum, Buena Park, Calif.

NASA Manned Spacecraft Center, Houston

National Safety Council

Naval Aviation Facilities Experimental Center, FAA

Naval Research Laboratory

North American Council of Telephone Pioneers

Pennsylvania Turnpike Commission

Queens Devices, Incorporated

Research Institute of Environ-
mental Medicine, U.S. Army
Smith Kline & French Laboratories
U.S. Atomic Energy Commission

U.S. Department of Army, Office of
Civil Defense
Walt Disney Productions
Wax Museum Enterprises

INDEX

113

116